This magnificent book is chock-full of Wilder's clever wit, wisdom, and raw humor. Laced with life-management counseling and sagacious insights, this is a "must read" for gutsy entrepreneurs, fast-track employees and all adventurous souls living on the "upside" of life!

Letty Herndon, President, Life Skills Collaborative, and Chair, Los Angeles Commission on the Status of Women Convention

The heart, interest and compassion that Judith has for showing others how to be successful is what this book has to share. And if you absorb her unselfish energy and intent, you can't help but shine! I know. I'm a grateful recipient of that energy and her unconditional gift of giving her knowledge and experience.

Raleigh Pinskey, author, "101 Ways To Promote Yourself" and "You Can Hype Anything"

Judith's humorous and witty approach to sharing real-life business advice and her wide array of experiences is a "must read" for any claimingly sane entrepreneur, artist, or business owner "Wannabe".

Forescee Hogan Rowles, Director, Community Financial Resource Center, Los Angeles

Judith writes from deep wisdom and broad experience with a witty, no-nonsense style. This book encourages the reader to aim high while simultaneously steering clear of the things one doesn't want to step into. The text only hints at the secrets of Judith's effectiveness and her gently forceful nature but the hints are useful ones.

Titus Levi, Ph.D, Assistant Professor, Annenberg School For Communication, University of Southern California

Fresh, funny, factual, filled with ideas and solutions . . .the best all around business guide and roadmap to success I've seen in years.

Adrienne Hall, President CEO, The Hall Group, and Commissioner, L.A. Commission on the Arts

DISCLAIMER
This book is designed to provide accurate and authoritative information in regard to the subject matter covered. It is sold with the understanding that neither the author nor publisher is engaged in rendering legal, accounting, or other professional services. If legal advice or other expert assistance is required, the services of a professional person should be sought.

National Network for Artist Placement, Los Angeles, California
Visit our Website at http://www.artistplacement.com

First Printing: November, 1999
10 9 8 7 6 5 4 3 2 1

Library of Congress Cataloging-in-Publication Data

Luther-Wilder, Judith.
     Breaking Through The Clutter/ Business Solutions for Women, Artists, and Entrepreneurs
     Includes Bibliographical References and a Resource Section.

ISBN 0-945941-11-0
1. Women owned business enterprises, United States.
2. Artists, United States.
3. Strategies for business success.

Copyright acknowledgments

The author gratefully acknowledges permission to reprint charts and information from "The Busy Woman's Guide To Successful Self-Employment", the "Bright Marketing Workbook", lists from the Association for Entrepreneurial Opportunity, Lawyers for the Arts, Accountants for the Public Interest and information from the United States Small Business Administration.

Cover design by Tyson Eckmeier. Lay out by Janet Trondle. Edited by Jeanie Barnett.

BREAKING THROUGH THE CLUTTER

Business Solutions for Women, Artists, and Entrepreneurs

By

Judith Luther Wilder

CONTENTS

Contents

Contents

Contents

DEDICATION

To Susan Richmond, Brian Toman, and Allison Sampson

There are 57 Rules for Success: first, deliver the goods. Second, the other 56 don't matter.

Author Unknown

FOREWORD

Once in a lifetime one finds a perch that provides access to some of the most extraordinary people in the world. My perch opened up when I was appointed National Director of the Office of Women's Business Ownership (OWBO) for the U.S. Small Business Administration. The position was as broad and inclusive as my title. I was in charge of all things done by the federal government to assist women entrepreneurs, a task that led from the White House to Congress and to cities across the country. Although it was a task that both inspired and frustrated, I will be forever grateful for my appointment because it led me to wonderful organizations in every state that had toiled for years to gain equity and access for the women who were changing the face of our nation's economy. It also introduced me to amazing individuals dedicated to improving the business environment for women-owned businesses, no matter how small or untraditional.

My future partner, Judith Luther Wilder, in 1990 the Director of one of the first Women's Business Centers funded by the SBA, was at the top of the list of extraordinary people I met during my tenure with OWBO. She not only had an ocean of experience she could relate with great humor but skills that helped us all navigate our way through the perilous waters that engulf most new programs in the early stages of development.

She brought an unusually practical perspective on small business and technical assistance to our field. In developing the California Center for the American Woman's Economic Development Corporation, she focused on providing people with the best resources to be successful and a chance to understand the mechanics of business without forcing them all to become accountants. With years as an artist and arts administrator under her belt, she understood that if you try to force creative people to mire themselves in the kind of bureaucratic detail that stupefies the best, you end up empowering the worst. Suffice it to say, this was not a goal for either of us nor in those days, even a goal of the federal government.

"Breaking Though The Clutter" addresses the challenge of doing business as a small or one-person shop where everything needs your attention simultaneously. It is a book that will make you laugh but it is also a book my colleagues at the Harvard Business School would do well to take to heart. Business schools must think more seriously about the realities small businesses face in this age of niche markets, sophisticated technology, and customers with high standards of service. It should certainly make artists who hope to turn their work, dreams and passion into a decent living think about "the business of art".

I hope it will also help smart Harvard MBA's give some thought to the "art of business".

Best of all, this book is primarily for and about women. To all those women who sat patiently through my speeches over the years, I can say without hesitation, "this is the book for you!" Enjoy.

Lindsey Johnson Suddarth, CEO, Women Incorporated

ORIGINS OF AN ENTREPRENEUR

If Head Parrothead Jimmy Buffet can tell his life story in four hundred words, I should be able to tell mine in five, give or take an adjective. Whether or not my story has any relevance to art or business remains to be seen but at the very least, it should serve as a signal that this is not about business as usual.

I was born on the Bay of Fundy in Nova Scotia, in a Godforsaken area I later came to view as the Appalachia of Canada. Like Appalachia, it had an inordinate number of desperately poor residents with bad teeth and it also had the kind of wonderful scenic beauty most urban dwellers cannot even imagine.

I left Nova Scotia when I was fifteen and ended up in Phoenix, Arizona, where I was almost instantly elected Girl's League President at Phoenix Union High School. I also was chosen to play Elaine in *Arsenic and Old Lace* and copped the female lead in Karel Capek's futuristic play, R.U.R. By any measure, my transition from a village of fifty fishermen and their families to a high school with five thousand teenagers obsessed with Chuck Berry, Jerry Lee Lewis and Elvis Presley had to be considered a success.

After graduating from high school, I took my award from the Daughters of the American Revolution (who apparently thought I was an American citizen), a $75 scholarship from the Association of Business and Professional Women and a typewriter one of my teachers had given me as a graduation gift, and high-tailed it to the University of Hawaii.

The Good News was that in 1958 out-of-state tuition at the University of Hawaii was $75 a semester. The Bad News was that I couldn't quite figure out the purpose of the registration queues nor manage to fill out the daunting sheaf of forms UH required of all incoming Freshman. After about three days of staring at the breathtaking double rainbows hanging over the campus and moving from one slow line to another, I left the campus and wandered down the hill to the Honolulu Academy of Arts. Under the ancient banyon tree in the Academy's front lawn, I found a Welcome mat, a folding table manned by a friendly art student and a one-page registration form even I could understand. I enrolled, gave them fifty of my $75, and remained at the Academy until my first son was born in 1960.

Between then and now I have visited, enjoyed and sometimes lingered in about twenty-five different countries, several of which were located in the Himalayas and a few of which were heavily land-mined. I have raised two sons (or possibly they have raised me), buried a husband, married another, found ten people I could love, four I could trust, and one who gave me $2.2 million to start a business. I have also managed a large municipal arts department and in the mid-'80s acquired a California Contractors License. In 1990, in a triumph of optimism over logic, I put aside my building blocks and took on the creation of a $5 million dollar international arts festival with opera director and Wild Child Peter Sellars. Since then I have opened the American Woman's Economic

1

Development Corporation in California, co-founded a company called Women Incorporated, received Ernst & Young's Entrepreneur of the Year Award, tanked a business, wrote a couple of books, bought a piece of land in Bali, and learned enough lessons about people, art, and entrepreneurism to fill a "How Not To" library.

This book is the result of all these experiences and if I write it properly, it will be helpful to you. If I write it badly, you can still use it for a resource guide, a paperweight or as a warning to young people who think they want to be artists or entrepreneurs.

Let the buyer beware.

GETTING STARTED

The person who said half the trick to succeeding in business is showing up is probably right. Simon and Schuster's Dick Snyder was fond of saying, *"It's better to be lucky than smart"* and he was also right. If you show up and you can manage to be smart <u>and</u> lucky, you have it licked.

My early businesses in Brighton, Nova Scotia, involved a lot of showing up and a certain amount of luck. They also often involved snaring or shooting something. When I was Executive Director of the American Woman's Economic Development Corporation, I was asked to write a short biography for a conference program and described my early efforts to snare rabbits. Sadly, when the program was printed, it described my regular efforts to snare a *rabbi*, a program note that was profoundly disturbing to the Jewish feminists I later had to address.

Most enterprising children growing up in Brighton trapped rabbits and sold their hides or shot squirrels and sold their tails. Today I'm sure this is politically incorrect even in Nova Scotia but in those days, I could get a nickel a tail and no one I ever knew paid much attention to the rights of squirrels. When you depend on deer meat and porcupine to get you through the winter, you tend to be insensitive to the rights of your furry friends.

During the summer months, when the Yankees and other tourists wandered across the border for their annual vacations, I curbed my bloodthirsty ways and turned to the arts as a means of making a fast buck. Purely by accident, I discovered I could paint a lighthouse to look like a lighthouse and a sailboat to look like the *Bluenose*. Within no time I was in touch with my artistic side and stockpiled an inventory of hand-painted scallop shells, rustic scenes painted prettily on driftwood, and flora and fauna painted on smooth rocks from St. Mary's Bay. I presided at every church fair, a dark-skinned child with big eyes and long braids, bartering happily with crazy tourists who seemed eager to pay as much as a quarter for the handiwork of a nine-year-old entrepreneur. In Brighton, Nova Scotia, at a time when the fisheries still paid men $20 a week for long hours of backbreaking labor, twenty-five cents for a shell you could pick off the beach was pretty big business.

Most people who lived around Digby and the Bay of Fundy were either fishermen, the wives or children of fishermen, employees at the fishmeal plant, farmers, or craftspeople. I doubt they thought of themselves as craftspeople any more than the fishermen thought of themselves as entrepreneurs, but it became apparent to me early on that it was a lot easier to make money painting clam shells than shucking them. Before I was ten, I was heavily into the Business of Art and I was also heavily motivated by the Art of Business. I loved to paint and I loved the fact that people would pay me to paint something for them. It was not until I was an adult living in America that it occurred to me the arts did not present an obvious money-making career path. Compared to fishing, where you're vulnerable to the vagaries of taste, pricing, weather, and frequent danger, quilting, carving and painting seashells seemed to me like a cushy way to make fast money.

The Balinese, people with whom I began to have a great deal of contact in the mid-'80's, may still share this view. Or as Neal Cassady said, "Art is good when it springs from necessity. This kind of origin is the guarantee of its value; there is no other."

What I learned from these early entrepreneurial experiences has held me in good stead as I have built, rebuilt, and expanded various businesses. Condensing my experience as an entrepreneurial artist/hunter in Brighton, Nova Scotia, this is what I learned:

- The materials for the product you sell may cost nothing more than the time it takes to collect them (but a Yankee tourist will never know that). And although you can charge the Yankee tourist a quarter for a scallop shell, Father D'Ambrose will make you say a hundred Hail Mary's if you try to charge your neighbor more than a nickel. Besides which you'll undoubtedly go to Hell.
- Two scallop shells are worth ten squirrel tails and the scallops are a lot tastier.
- If you wear your hair loose and your dress is always clean, you earn more than if you wear braids and your brother's dirty work pants.
- Always smile and thank customers who don't buy from you. It doesn't cost you anything and it will either make the customer feel good or bad. Both of which work for you.
- Yankee tourists don't want to listen to you. They want you to listen to them. This is probably true of most tourists and most customers. And most husbands. Never miss a good chance to say nothing.
- Give regular customers a free squirrel's tail now and then. It makes them feel good and the squirrel is already dead.

And while I didn't learn the following in Nova Scotia, I agree wholeheartedly with the tall Texan who said, "*Good judgment comes from experience and a lot of that comes from bad judgment.*"

Which is why you should read on and Do As I Say, Not As I Did.

ATTITUDE

You can't overestimate the value of a good attitude. I have worked with highly successful people with no visible talents who were golden simply because they had great attitudes. I have hired people because they convinced me they were cheerful, low-maintenance, and showed evidence of a good work ethic. I have not hired obviously talented people that sent convincing signals they had bad or at least troublesome attitudes.

Curiously, job applicants and potential collaborators often tell you straight out they are perfectionists and a pain in the butt. They actually boast about taking the bull by the horns and confronting people immediately when even slightly irritated by something or someone in their work environment. While I do not think there is anything inherently wrong with confrontational people who call a spade a spade, I just do not want a lot of them around me. Particularly if they IMMEDIATELY tell you when they are upset. I prefer to surround myself with people who think about a problem for a few hours or days before they verbally destroy someone who intended no offense. A little stoicism in the workplace is not an entirely bad thing.

For the purpose of this discussion and this book, I define someone with a great attitude as a person who

- Never whines
- Does not expect a free ride or a free lunch
- Is not thin skinned and does not take himself too seriously
- Does not assume the world is obsessed with cheating him personally
- Does not spend a lot of time trashing other people, and
- Does not look for trouble.

A person with a great attitude is someone who

- Works hard and enjoys it
- Has integrity
- Is joyous and laughs at herself more often than she laughs at others
- Actually listens when others are speaking
- Enjoys the good fortune of others
- Shows up on time, and
- Is as low-maintenance as it is humanly possible to be.

People with great attitudes may also, on very rare occasions, sport stiff upper lips but if the stiff upper lips ever evolve into martyrdom, they cross the Good Attitude Border and merely end up wandering aimlessly in the Land of Bad Attitudes. Martyrs are only a quiet variation of people with bad attitudes and they are always a pain in the neck to be around. In addition to an absence of good problem solving skills, their creativity gene is usually missing. Can you imagine living with Joan of Arc? Every time there was a problem, she'd whistle the same old tiresome tune ("Louie, Louie") and run off to New Orleans to round up defectors from the French Foreign Legion.

I am fortunate to know a lot of people with good to great attitudes, several of whom paid me to work for them and several that have worked for me. They have not always been the most scholarly people in the Universe but they have always been effective and sure as Hell were a lot of fun to be around. Except when shopping for a brain surgeon, at this stage of my life I will always trade a creative genius with a bad attitude for a good-humored, hard-working, personally secure employee with a great attitude.

On the other side of the fence, there are People From Hell with attitudes that range between bizarre and psychotic. Patti Koltnow is the owner of Koltnow & Associates and the interim CEO of a large Los Angeles non-profit organization. She is also a friend and colleague who put the capital G and A in Good Attitude and has a whole collection of stories about People From Hell. Originally her collection featured only Women From Hell but by the time she'd been "dissed" by 110 BMW owners, she decided she should not be gender specific.

Her files include women with the worst credit in recorded history, many of whom would call her when she worked at Women Incorporated to demand immediate loans. If she couldn't deliver bushel baskets of low interest money to them within the hour, they'd berate her, insult every member of her family and usually threaten to report her to every regulatory agency in the country. Generally the women who called were sole proprietors that, when questioned about their most recent bankruptcies, would say with great indignation, "But those were *personal* bankruptcies. I'm requesting a *business* loan and I've never had a *business* bankruptcy." She also includes in her distressingly large People From Hell file tales about Board members who never attend Board meetings, never sign up for committee work and never contribute in any visible way to the well-being of the organizations they represent. These are invariably the same people who are front and center and near the microphone when the Governor, a Hollywood star, or a major donor drops by.

Women clearly have no monopoly on bad manners or hot-dogging. Ask any refugee from a Fortune 500 company, any career military man, anyone who works in Silicon Valley or for NASA and anyone who ever worked on a movie set with the latest Hunk of the Month. Bad Attitudes are equal opportunity afflictions.

Patti probably takes these kinds of offenses to heart more than most of us because she is such an extraordinarily reasonable and sane person. Most of the time. Although I can't say she never complains, I have only heard her complain about other complainers, abusive people and BMW owners. In a decade of working together, I've never heard her lament about working conditions, poor health, inconvenience, or anything related to her workload. And she's had every right to do so. She's worked in neighborhoods that hardened felons avoid. She's worked for organizations that spoke no English (she speaks only English) and in one instance, had no written language. She's worked for poor and sometimes no pay and she's worked with people who were abusive and demanding. As far as I can tell, she scarcely noticed working conditions that would make most players in the NFL quake. But put her next to a BMW owner on the freeway and she instantly needs an attitude adjustment.

BMW owners are, to Patti, the living personification of People With Attitude (all Bad). She and her husband, Barry, a very funny man who writes a syndicated column called "Barrywood", have conducted a fifteen-year study trying to determine if only assholes buy BMWs or if buying BMWs turns them into assholes. To date they have reached no conclusion but if you ask them to list their top ten categories of people with Bad Attitudes, BMW owners beat out Slobodan Milosevic. Her top ten list also includes people who make a major production out of a simple job assignment, people who sue because their coffee is lukewarm or because someone hurt their feelings, and anyone who avoids accountability.

With BMW owners at the pinnacle, she and I have put together an All Star List of Bad Attitude Bad Asses no one should ever hire. I have also developed a Top Ten List of People With Good Attitudes who should not only be hired but cloned. Or brought back to life if they have sadly exhausted their ability to breathe, be cheerful, joyous, and prompt.

Our All Star List of Bad Attitude Bad Asses

1.   the much maligned BMW owners (explanation given above)
2.   a tie between Idi Amin, Adolph Hitler, Slobodon Milosevic and Pol Pot (no explanation necessary)
3.   Medea (poor problem solver)
4.   Lawrence Durrell (wrote like an angel; behaved like a devil)
5.   Bill Clinton (blamed the Right Wing when he was caught with his pants down. On national television. Twice.)
6.   Ken Starr (no sense of humor. Mean bastard. Missed the point.)
7.   Ellen De Generes (talented, funny, rich and needs to acknowledge her show was cancelled because it was boring)
8. 92% of the people who served in Congress in 1998 (no explanation necessary)
9.   Artists and athletes with bad manners who can't seem to remember average people in the United States haul in an annual salary of $33,000 AND THEY WORK THEIR ASSES OFF FOR IT.
10. Career bureaucrats who wield power like petty tyrants in Third World countries propped up by a military force the U.S. has trained and armed, commonly found in DMV, IRS, and EDD offices throughout the country.

My Top Ten List of People With Good Attitudes (on which Patti gets a free ride)

1.   Mother Teresa (worked in the heat in a bad neighborhood, had a terrible wardrobe and dry skin and always managed a beatific smile)
2.   Dalai Lama (has to put up with Richard Gere, wear orange-colored sheets, pass up Prime Rib and doesn't have a Potala to pee in. Still manages to be jolly.)

3. Katherine Hepburn (always worked hard, was seldom tardy and never appeared to sweat the small stuff)
4. Bill Viola (unpretentious MacArthur Genius grantee who takes his work and his wife more seriously than he takes himself. Role model for artists who think suffering may be a substitute for talent.)
5. James Carville (ugly son-of-a-bitch with enough energy to jump start Hoover Dam. Doesn't let politics get in the way of his life. Or his wife.)
6. Several of the women who have lived with my complicated and sometimes difficult sons (an explanation would be imprudent)
7. Father Gregory Boyle and Ron Noblet (two East Los Angeles gang workers who can still laugh at themselves after laboring for decades on the mean streets of Los Angeles but who NEVER GAVE UP!)
8. The 1999 World Cup Champion United States Women's Soccer Team (poster girls for Title IX and the sports bra industry)
9. Ann Richards (former Governor of Texas who is actually funny and didn't look for someone to blame when she lost the state to George Jr.)
10. Arthur Ashe (no explanation necessary)

Regrettably, I cannot put myself on the Top Ten or even Top 100 List of People With Good Attitudes. Although I am certainly always prompt and spend a fair amount of time laughing at myself, this book will document my readiness to complain about or at least criticize my fellow men and women. I also would like a free ride with a free lunch thrown in. I would like to win the Lotto when the pot is really big. I'd like a MacArthur Grant although I'd prefer they give it to me for above average intelligence rather than insisting on genius. And I would like a pill that would make me thin and fit and would leave me looking ten years younger without ever having to sign up for a tummy tuck, a face lift, or liposuction.

Rachel Bellow, the incorrigible Director of Project 180 in New York, says I am the kind of person who will call for and expect to get a glass of ice water when I'm burning in Hell. Which more or less disqualifies me from all Top Ten lists.

Nonetheless, I still maintain that I don't belong on any serious list of people with Bad Attitudes. I have enough of the Catholic Nova Scotian left in me to remember it is a mortal sin to whine about hard work or bad luck. I love to work hard when hard work is called for, I like to play hard when it's time to play, I understand and accept that "shit happens" to everyone and I would much rather listen than talk. Providing the person speaking to me isn't a talking squash with a bad attitude. In which case, I merely pretend to listen and mentally plan my next vacation. So while I am not likely to end up in Patti's People From Hell Files, Mother Teresa and Katherine Hepburn have nothing to fear from me. Their places in the Good Attitude Hall of Fame are secure.

To cut to the chase, the thing for an employer or business owner to remember when hiring is this: Talent is random and perfectly awful people often have it coming out their evil ears. I'm not suggesting that you hire a good-humored and unskilled boob but I am suggesting you run, not walk, from anyone you suspect is temperamental or who habitually sends $3 glasses of wine back to the bar hoping they will be replaced by a vintage bottle of Pouilly Fuisse.

A good work ethic and a sense of humor are invaluable and integrity and a generous spirit are qualities angels probably envy. When you have a chance to hire someone or if you are choosing a partner with whom you anticipate a long period of collaboration, always go for competence but pay special attention to the girl (or guy) with the gusto.

They will make you rich and simultaneously enrich your life.

ARTISTS AND ENTREPRENEURS

Art for art's sake is a philosophy of the well-fed.

Yu Cao

Trying to make a living in one job while pursuing a bigger and often nobler dream is a dilemma faced by both artists and entrepreneurs. To pay the bills and support a family, artists often end up employed as bookkeepers, waiters, teachers, carpenters, cab drivers and lawyers. Entrepreneurs also end up working two or even three jobs to support their passions. "Don't quit your day job!" say the parents, friends and spouses of artists and entrepreneurial "wannabe's". When the artists and would-be entrepreneurs have families depending on the income they generate, that advice has to be taken seriously.

During the course of writing this book, sixty artists and thirty-five women entrepreneurs were interviewed or surveyed. Of the ninety-five, all were driven by a powerful passion to do work that was more creative, to create beauty or to achieve economic independence for themselves and their families. Without exception they had all made significant sacrifices to hold onto their dreams and no one had a trust fund or wealthy patrons to see them through their lean years.

The failure rate for entrepreneurs is very high (only one in every fifteen survives longer than three years) but those that survived fared better financially than the artists my associates and I interviewed. Although not as well educated (fifty of the sixty artists interviewed had advanced degrees), the average entrepreneur earned three times as much as the average artist at the five-, ten- and twenty-year career point. This accomplishment is particularly impressive because over half the entrepreneurs we interviewed suffered dramatic business failures during the first three years of starting their businesses and had to begin anew.

Entrepreneurs

Debi Davis, the founder of Fit America, used a Rolex watch, her only valuable possession, as collateral for the $5,000 she needed to get her business started in 1991. By 1993 she was able to buy back her Rolex and last year her 60 stores across the country brought in about $33 million.

A home economist with two daughters, Doris Christopher started the Pampered Chef, a business that earned $500 million in 1998, with $3,000 she borrowed on a life-insurance policy. Kitchen shears, a few garlic presses, and some lumber for her basement office were the only items and materials she could afford when she began her business. Eventually she created an impressive product line and developed a huge sales force of 42,000 independent sales representatives. For the first couple of years, however, her one-woman business depended exclusively on word-of-mouth marketing and her own drive and vision.

Steve Peskaitis, the 23-year-old president of Chicago Map Corporation, says he learned to play monopoly before he could read. When he was fifteen, he borrowed $500 from his Dad for 100 CD-ROMs loaded with "shareware". Until the big companies discovered his niche, he sold the CDs for $70 each at computer conventions. In 1992 he opened another business that specialized in DOS-interactive street maps on CD-ROMs. This time he sold 20,000 copies for $69 each but his success was once again short-lived. When Microsoft entered the picture, he moved away from the consumer market and began licensing mapping technology to software firms that create a variety of applications.

His goal, says Peskaitis, is "to become the digital Rand McNally." If everything stays on track, his company will bring in $5 million in 1999.

Not all the entrepreneurs we surveyed were millionaires. Yolanda Mendiveles, a massage therapist who has been self-employed for twelve years, has deliberately kept her business small.

When Yolanda was first licensed, she kept her job as a chemical dependency counselor and also ran a small commercial and residential cleaning business. As her massage business grew, she gained the confidence she needed to leave her position as a social worker, and eventually sold her cleaning business.

By the time she developed her massage business into a full time job, she discovered that a lot of her colleagues with heavy workloads were experiencing work-related injuries. In addition, she realized her clients were not getting the kind of service she had envisioned giving and she scaled her work week back to half-time. This enabled her to provide her clients with extremely personalized service. She could accommodate their schedules on weekends or in the evening and she could provide the kind of care and attention that distinguished her from other massage therapists.

Simultaneously, her decreased work schedule provided her with a better quality of life. Although she makes less than $30,000 a year, she has time to take classes in other subjects that interest her. In the five years since we met, Yolanda has taken voice lessons, astrology, ceramics and a basic electronics class. She has also spent three months in England studying writing, six months in Colorado working on a play and has traveled to Macchu Picchu, Peru, with a group of psychic healers. Not bad for someone who works part time.

Her annual salary is a little misleading because she also barters her services for haircuts, advertising, printing and even computer equipment. The reason she took the electronics class, she says, was so she could maintain and repair a computer a client had given her in exchange for massages. Other loyal clients make sure she gets right of first refusal when they need housesitters for their luxurious homes.

Still, unlike most entrepreneurs, Yolanda is not driven by a need for financial gain so much as a need for independence and control over her time. In this regard, her motivations are probably more akin to those of artists than to business owners. Her lifestyle is very modest and by the standards of many middle-class consumers, she travels very light.

She appears, however, more satisfied with the life she's designed for herself than many business owners with multi-million dollar businesses and houses full of creature comforts. She is a particular kind of entrepreneur, neither commonplace nor uncommon, but a type rarely profiled in Entrepreneur or Working Woman magazines. As self-employment increases, and it will, we'll see many more Yolandas who place a high value on leisure time and want to control their own destinies.

Artists

I'm convinced that artists, like entrepreneurs, are born rather than developed through training or education. Education and training help everyone but the tolerance for risk and the drive to be an artist or business owner may come with the original equipment at birth. The creativity gene is also undoubtedly in the original package, as is the ability to stick it out through thick and thin. If our surveys have any validity, artists and entrepreneurs are proof positive that tenacity counts.

Bill Viola, the brilliant video artist and MacArthur Fellow/Getty Scholar whose work has been exhibited in museums and galleries all over the world, says he did not make a living from his art until 1995, twenty-two years after he graduated from art school. Judith Baca, the founder of SPARC and one of the premiere muralists in the country, says she has never made a living from either her murals or paintings. John Outterbridge, the gifted artist who served as the Director of Watts Towers from 1975 to 1992, says that his museum and gallery exhibitions have never supported him. He once had a one-man show at Brockman Gallery in Los Angeles that sold out and earned more than $20,000 for him and Alonzo Davis, the gallery owner, but this was a once-in-a-lifetime experience.

According to John, his " true pay-off over the years is to finally discover the making of art equates to the practicing of one's life." Bill Viola echoes John's sentiments when he remarks "Art lives outside museums and galleries. Your life experiences are your art."

Fortunately, all three artists have always been able to support themselves and their work with artists' residencies, teaching, lectures, and art-related work. They are also dedicated to making their work at all costs. "Protect the precious jewel that is your expression," says John Outterbridge.

"Success comes from the inner creative process and commitment to working," adds Viola. "Do whatever you can to survive. Broaden your experiences early on – every situation contains a teaching and can be useful later even if it is not apparent at the time," he observes. He also facetiously says he is urging his two sons to become investment bankers so they can support their parents in their old age.

All artists are not able or willing to work in an arts-related field. While teaching, administration and lecturing has worked for Baca, Viola and Outterbridge, other artists are more comfortable doing work they don't have to think about when they go home at night. Which may be why Phillip Glass once worked as a cab driver, Harrison Ford as a carpenter, and Karen Atkinson as a cook who prepared meals for 1,000 people per day. The need to save their energy and passion for their art may also account, together with fear of hunger, for the hundreds of actors in Los Angeles and New York who work as waiters, bus boys, bartenders and cocktail waitresses.

The Waitress Turned Super Star Myth notwithstanding, fewer artists today work in the restaurant industry than most people suppose. A 1994 survey conducted by KPMG Peat Marwick and the California Arts Council showed that the stereotype of the starving artist working as a poorly paid busboy or waitress was an inaccurate reflection of California artists. According to their report, artists in California are highly educated people who, in 1994, earned an average of $38,000. The survey showed they were involved in their communities to a greater extent than the average citizen, 86% voted, 50% were volunteers and 74% contributed to charity. Although some did have second jobs in the restaurant and hotel industries, far more worked as part-time teachers, lawyers and paralegals, financial advisors and arts administrators.

"The starving artist bit is a myth," says Suzanna Guzman, an opera singer who has performed at the Metropolitan Opera, the Kennedy Center and Carnegie Hall. Although $6,000 is the most she's ever made for a performance, her part-time work as an office manager, a camp counselor and a movie extra has enabled her to afford the classes, lessons, and training she needed to be competitive. "Being a performing artist is a business," says the well-known mezzo-soprano, "as well as a vocation."

With an aunt who ran the Los Angeles Marathon for the first time when she was seventy years old, Suzanna knows something about preparing for the long haul. The East Los Angeles girl who now plays roles such as Carmen in some of the most prestigious opera houses in the world, says with conviction, "You must do your art to reach your own personal best and not measure success by how much money you make or what others think. Art is an individual's quest for expression and you should pursue that quest with all your heart. If it keeps a roof over your head and food on the table, great! If it doesn't, do something else. Just don't give up. Keep on trying until you're where you want to be."

Artists who start businesses as a second career tend to fare less well in business than their non-artist business colleagues. Not realizing that business ownership is as demanding a mistress as art, artists often enter into an entrepreneurial endeavor with an unrealistic picture of what it takes to succeed.

Unlike Yolanda Mendiveles, entrepreneurs driven by passion and profit find themselves spending more time and energy on building their own businesses than they ever spent on a job for another employer. In order to make a business thrive, the business owner needs to devote as much drive to his enterprise as an artist devotes to his art. Artists/business owners usually opt *not* to dedicate their passion and time to the business they created to support their art. Logically, they devote less focus and psychic energy to their businesses than they do to their primary passion, to their choreography, their sculpture or their music, and they risk far less. Consequently, they avoid the spectacular failures their business colleagues experience but they also fail to achieve the brilliant successes of a Doris Christopher or a Steve Peskaitas.

Still, many of the artists surveyed for this book maintain a belief in the importance of understanding business. Visual artist/sculptor Gilbert "Magu" Lujan advises young artists to "be informed, be business comprehensive and plan with financial clarity". He also suggests that they "not do as I did. Learn from others," he says, "work hard at what you do and do your best."

Jeweler/sculptor Karen McCreary, a twenty-year art world veteran, tells young artists to "keep an open mind about the many ways your art skills can be used in the marketplace. While developing your artistic skills, do not ignore other important business skills such as marketing, contracts, and self-promotion."

Karen, who has worked as a sales clerk and in accounting for many years, says she's "still working on making a living from her art".

Tina Spiro, an inspired painter who runs a gallery in Jamaica and buys Cuban art for collectors in South Florida, recommends that someone starting out in the arts today should not rely on sales of their work. "Start an arts-related business," she says. "It's better to earn a living at something related to art rather than to commercialize your work and drop your standards."

Director Becky Bristow, currently director of The Wild Thornberrys at Klasky/Csupo Productions, and former chair of Character Animation at the California Institute of the Arts, has always been able to support herself through her work as an animator. She recommends that young artists go to a studio and beg for any job they can get. "At Klasky/Csupo," she says, "people with talent come in and accept the lowest-paying jobs just to break into the industry. In a relatively short period of time, they usually move into a more creative position within the company."

Building a business can also enable an artist to maintain his artistic integrity. John Sanders, a sculptor who graduated from art school in 1972, runs the Mar Mel Bed and Breakfast for Dogs & Cats in Long Beach, California. "Unless you're lucky, you will have to support your work yourself," he says. "Income from your art is irregular but if you have a business, you don't have to compromise your ideas for money."

Workplace experts recommend that young artists find jobs that appeal to secondary interests. "A lot of creative types are multi-talented," says Susan Abbot, owner of Abbot & Co., a San Francisco firm that specializes in career counseling for creative and unconventional people.

Heeding her advice, actor Michael Brady turned his skydiving hobby into a weekend job as a skydiving instructor. Figurative painter Parnell Corder works as a makeup artist during the day. "I'm painting on a face rather than a canvas but I'm still creating a look, a work of art in some way," he says. Chris Hardman, an interdisciplinary performance artist and the artistic director/founder of Antenna Inc., turned his "Walkmanology" experiments into an artistic medium by applying Walkmanology principles to museum exhibitions. Museums that installed Antenna's audio tours include the Art Institute of Chicago, the Los Angeles County Museum of Art, and the Seattle Art Museum.

Novelist Marc Laidlaw, who says he was a "human parasite" the first five years of his career, has also worked as a legal secretary and now has a high-paying writing job for a company that develops video games. The corporations for which he's worked as a secretary have been "boring," he says, "but they pay well." According to Marc, who is the author of six books, including *Neon Lotus* and *Dad's Nuke*, "Even simple typing jobs enable writers to practice. Make the most you can make with your skills," says the busy father of two pre-schoolers, "and keep doing your art in your copious spare time."

Staying Healthy

Even more than people in other professions, artists and entrepreneurs recognize how critical it is to stay healthy. Because many artists cannot afford dental and health insurance, they work harder at maintaining their health than other professionals who take health insurance programs for granted. Women entrepreneurs also have a great awareness of the hazards of being unable to work. Veterans of low-paying jobs with few benefits, many of them single parents, they've developed a keen sense of how important it is to provide health insurance for their own employees. This awareness is reflected in a 1999 study conducted by the National Foundation for Women Business Owners. According to its report, women business owners are more likely than men entrepreneurs to provide health insurance, flex time and support for childcare programs.

"Exercise regularly. Take care of your health. Keep 'drama' out of your daily life and avoid unhealthy individuals who are self-imploding," says Denise Uyehara, a performance artist/playwright.

"Be strong, be healthy," says Suzanna Guzman, doubtless speaking both as a parent and as an artist who recognizes she is her own instrument.

Dancers, even more than other artists, are concerned not only about their health but also about staying extraordinarily fit. The language they speak is a difficult one to learn and they pay a heavy price for their fluency. From the beginning of their careers to the end, they struggle with fatigue, pain, injuries and a clock that can't be stopped. Forty-year-old dancers may be more insightful, expressive and disciplined than their twenty-year-old colleagues but their bodies also require more rest, more care and more inspirational peptalks.

Fred Strickler, a concert dancer for whom symphonic orchestras often commission new work, co-founded Jazz Tap Ensemble over twenty years ago. Still dancing *beautifully*, Fred says, "Keep in mind that more than ninety percent of people who have dance careers are finished by the age of thirty-five and forty. You <u>have</u> to stay healthy."

As a dancer, his observations about a second career are also interesting. "You have to think, even at eighteen," he says, "about what else you can do to support yourself. Develop something else. Find something else you can do to make money. Perhaps a business skill or something that allows you flexible hours. Because dancing is not economically viable for ninety-five percent of the dancers in the country, you have to find another work skill that will be both interesting and pay the bills.

"Broaden yourself in all the arts. Familiarize yourself with art history, with contemporary art forms, with visual arts and with video. Learn to read music. If you are a choreographer, it's a great advantage. Get involved. Go to the theater, go to films. Familiarize yourself with the society in which you're working. Remember art does not exist in a vacuum. Get involved with your community. Don't isolate yourself by being an artist in a hothouse studio. There *are* distinct advantages to having your own studio and working on your own vision but if your vision as an artist is not bigger than yourself, it's not a very big vision," says the elder statesman of tap.

Like entrepreneurs concerned about producing the best product or best service, Fred, as did other artists we interviewed, expresses a commitment to standards and quality. "When you ask an audience to sit in front of you for an evening or even ten minutes," he says, "I think it behooves you to do your best. There is just too little opportunity to perform. When you go out on that stage, do your best. If you do that, you'll always be satisfied. I've done self-indulgent work and it just doesn't work. What happens is that the references are so internalized that nobody can connect with it. Dancing is a language of communication and if you're going to communicate, communicate. Don't expect your audience to work nearly as hard as you would like them to in order to understand your art. Just give."

"The best dancers," says Strickler, "are always givers!"

Finally, a quote from the late and incomparable Margot Fonteyn, a dancer who knew a little bit about the business of art: *"The one important thing I have learned over the years is the difference between taking one's work seriously and taking one's self seriously. The first is imperative and the second is disastrous."*

However you define success, successful artists and successful entrepreneurs appear to be united in taking their work very seriously and in taking themselves with a healthy grin and grain of salt. They are not-so-distant cousins with a profound understanding of passion, commitment, sacrifice and the joy of dreaming very large dreams.

NOTES

FINANCIAL PLANNING FOR ARTISTS, WOMEN ENTREPRENEURS AND OTHERS WHO DO NOT THINK THE TAX MAN IS THEIR FRIEND

The education most of us receive in college does not include an introduction to bookkeeping, tax preparation or how to prepare a Statement of Profit and Loss. Art schools certainly do not do a good job of preparing artists to manage the business side of their careers. Even the revered Harvard Business School, according to my partner and Harvard Business School alum, Lindsey Johnson Suddarth, does not adequately prepare their students to master practical tasks such as business tax preparation and computing withholding tax.

It is clear to me that far too many educational institutions encourage their graduates to invest bookkeepers and accountants with too much power. Even if the scope of your business dictates that you contract professional bookkeeping services, you should understand what you are getting for your money. Although many of us treat it as such, bookkeeping is not a mystery only CPAs can unravel.

Record Keeping

The best bookkeeping system is the simplest bookkeeping system you can understand and manage. If you can't understand your own record keeping system and you find you are spending more than three hours a week on bookkeeping, your system is too complicated or your business is big enough to warrant professional assistance.

Your most important reasons for keeping good records are to

- Determine how much your business is earning or losing and
- To account to the government for both your income and expenditures.

One of the most effective and easiest bookkeeping systems I have ever heard or read about was recommended in an old book (now out of print) written by photographer Jeanne Thwaites. In her book entitled *"Starting And Succeeding In Your Own Photography Business"*, she suggests reducing your bookkeeping system to three ledgers and a spike. A spike is a weighted base with a spike sticking upwards and is used to hold receipts and other information until you have time to record or file it in one of three ledgers.

In order to save time, buy ledgers that are uniform in size but are in different colors so that you can identify them quickly. Use an ink or ballpoint pen for all your record keeping. Black ink is preferable in case you need to photocopy your records. Do not use a pencil if you want the IRS to take you seriously.

In Ledger I you will record the date you received income, the amount and its source. Whether you do anything else will depend on what you want to accomplish with your bookkeeping. As you expand your business, you may discover a need for additional information but be wary of unnecessary record keeping or duplication.

Ledger II is for your receivables. In this ledger you should record the date of your business transaction, the person or company to whom you sold an item or provided a service, their address, the amount owed, and the billing date or status of the account (e.g. the account went to Collections on 8/14/98).

Ledger III is used to keep track of all the money you spend. Record what you spend, when you spend, where your money goes, the amount of the expenditure and whether you paid for it by check or with cash.

The spike simply serves as a temporary file for all the receipts and bills you don't have time to immediately record in your ledgers.

Your checking account is a good back up for Ledger III. If you lose some of your receipts, which the IRS will demand as proof of purchase, your cancelled checks can serve as back-up receipts.

If a simple Three Ledgers and a Spike system is too simple for your needs and sensibilities, try one of the many computer software packages for record keeping sold in every Office Depot, Staples or Office Max outlet.

Since most small businesses fail because of cash flow problems, you need to be particularly careful about monitoring your expenditures. You will be able to determine an appropriate price for what you sell by keeping track of what you spend and how much you sell. You may also discover you are spending too much on items that do not contribute to the service you provide or the product you sell. By overspending on items that do not contribute to either the creation or the sale of your work, you may deprive yourself in ways that eventually force you out of business. Keeping good records will give you the information you need to analyze where you're going and how much it is costing you to get there.

Tax Preparation

While it is both realistic and desirable for you as a self-employed person to oversee your own bookkeeping, it is very important to hire an accountant to prepare your tax returns. Tax laws change so quickly you will be hard pressed to keep abreast of the changes. Even with today's "kinder, gentler" IRS, you may get yourself in trouble if you insist on being your own accountant. At best, you may cheat yourself out of many profitable and legitimate deductions.

If you can't afford to hire an accountant, you may locate one who will work at a greatly reduced fee or will trade services with your company.

Accountants for the Public Interest have a number of affiliate offices throughout the country. A list is included in the Resource Section. If there is not an office near you, call one of the affiliates and ask to be referred to an accountant who does volunteer consulting in your city. Many state branches of the Society of Certified Public Accountants also have public service committees that can provide you with the assistance you need.

If you still do not believe that hiring an accountant will save you a ton of money or help you avoid ruin and humiliation, consult one of several excellent guides on the market for people who insist on doing things the hard way. *"The Art of Deduction"*, prepared by the Bay Area Lawyers for the Arts; *"The Art of Filing"*, by Carla Messman; and *"Fear of Filing: A Beginner's Guide To Tax Preparation and Record Keeping For Artists, Performers, Writers and Free Lance Professionals"* by Theodore W. Striggles, are all designed to help you stay in the good graces of They Who Must Be Obeyed, the IRS.

Other good books that may save you from financial disaster include the following:

"Tax Planning and Preparation Made Easy for the Self-Employed" by Gregory L. Dent and Jeffery E. Johnson
"Minding Her Own Business: The Self-Employed Woman's Guide to Taxes and Recordkeeping" by Jan Zobel
"Don't Let the IRS Destroy Your Small Business: Seventy Six Mistakes To Avoid" by Michael Savage

Some Basic Information You Will Need To Keep The IRS And Other Tax Agencies Happy

Keeping the IRS happy is a noble goal but it's probably easier to quit smoking and maintain a twenty-inch waistline. You may, however, manage to stay out of trouble if you adhere to their top 1,297 rules, regulations and recommendations, a few of which are included in the following paragraphs:

If you receive more than $400 in any calendar year from an individual or a company, you should expect to receive a Form 1099-MISC. If you pay someone $400 or more in a calendar year, you must issue that person a Form 1099-MISC indicating exactly how much you paid them. The 1099-MISC form comes in three parts. Copies are sent to both the recipient of the money and to the government. The payer keeps the third copy as proof of deductions on her Schedule C.

When hiring employees, have them fill out Form 1-9 and Form W-4. After the calendar year is over, furnish copies of Form W-2, *Wage and Tax Statement*, to each employee to whom you paid wages during the year. You must also send copies to the Social Security Administration.

As a self-employed person, you will at least need to file Form 1040, Schedules C and SE and possibly Forms 4562 and 3468. If you purchased business equipment in the preceding year, you must indicate this on Forms 4562 and 3468. If you own your own home, you should itemize personal deductions on Schedule A. If you are married to a working spouse, you will also need a Schedule W and if you paid for childcare while you worked, you will need Form 2441.

Begin preparing your federal returns with Schedule C. This document consists of four sections: an Introduction plus Part I (which deals with income); Part II provides space to list your deduction and Part III determines the cost of goods sold in your business.

You can obtain all the forms you need from your nearest federal building or from most post offices. If these buildings are not conveniently located, write the federal government and request a complete packet of all necessary forms. You can also request forms and information through the IRS website at www.ustreas.gov or at www.taxkit.com.

Keep track of all reports such as interest payments, 1099-MISC forms, and statements of dividends. Set the reports aside in a manila envelope marked Record of Miscellaneous Income and turn the envelope over to your accountant at tax time.

As a self-employed person, you are also required to make quarterly estimated tax payments to cover your annual tax liability. From your last tax payment, estimate the amount of tax you expect to pay in the current year. Divide that amount by four and make your first quarterly payment by April 15. The second payment is due in mid-June, the third in mid-September and the fourth on January 15. In order to avoid a costly interest charge, always pay at least as much each year as the previous year's total tax.

Some examples of expenses that, as of the date of publication, can be legitimately deducted from your income in order to reduce your taxes are:

- Business Start-Up Costs such as a business license, business cards, advertising, office equipment or machinery
- Business Use of Your Home if your home is your principal place of business, a place where you regularly meet with clients and/or a separate structure you use in connection with your trade or business
- Rent if you multiply your rent payments by the percentage of your home used for business
- Cost of repairs and supplies that relate to your business
- Utilities and services (the business percentage of your utilities is the same as the percentage of your home used for business)
- Telephone charges on dedicated business lines or for long distance business calls made on a personal phone line
- Travel to business meetings or to conferences related to your business
- Mileage if you use your car for business. Use actual costs or the Standard Mileage Rate. In 1998, the cost for operating your car for business was 32 ½ cents per mile.

These are only a few examples of expenses that can be deducted with impunity. Although tax laws may treat artists and self-employed people as both individual income earners and sole proprietorships, they also provide special benefits self-employed people are in a unique position to enjoy.

Do not forget to pay your Self-Employment Tax. The self-employment tax on net earnings is 15.3%, a total of 12.4% for social security and 2.9% for Medicare. All net earnings of at least $400 are subject to Medicare charges.

Find an accountant that has worked with other artists and self-employed people and has a reputation for being scrupulously honest. Once a qualified accountant has guided you through an encounter with the IRS, you won't want to go back to personally second-guessing government auditors.

If you are audited, call NADN.

NADN stands for the National Audit Defense Network, a nationwide network of nearly 1000 former IRS agents, auditors, CPAs and tax attorneys who have switched sides and now work on behalf of the taxpayer. To reach a NADN representative, call 1-800-AWAY IRS or e mail them at awayirs@awayirs.com.

Prepare for all dealings with the IRS as carefully as you would prepare for a meeting with the Pope or the Queen of England. Remember that the money you earn and keep is as valuable as additional earned income. A Supreme Court decision has given every taxpayer the right to arrange her affairs so that she can pay the least amount of tax. Take advantage of this and hold on to as many of your hard-earned dollars as the law allows.

NOTES

THE GRANTSMANSHIP GAME

A good grant proposal is to the non-profit world what a good business plan is to the for-profit world. Both documents, if done well, will tell an investor about your ability to plan, the strength of your staff, your target market, your financial operations, and the extent to which you have your act together.

Conversely, when poorly organized and written, grant proposals will tell prospective donors that the quality of your programs is uneven, your Board of Directors lacks commitment, your organization is poorly managed and that you wouldn't know how to read a balance sheet if you had one tattooed on your thigh.

A proposal outline designed by a foundation that distributes millions of grant dollars annually is included at the end of this chapter. If you are only interested in finding out the kinds of information conventional funders require from grant applicants, skip the next few pages. This chapter deals primarily with what goes on before and after you have filled in the blanks and submitted it to a wise and godlike staff and/or panel for review.

Grants for Individual Artists

Since most foundation funding is awarded to non-profit organizations, individual artists will need to do a lot of research to identify funding sources for their discipline. Remember that foundation provisions for individual grants usually require advance approval by the IRS. Although you may want them to tailor their guidelines for your specific request, grantmakers cannot make exceptions to the guidelines the IRS has approved.

The Foundation Center publishes two publications that may cut your research time in half. The *11th Edition of Foundation Grants To Individuals* features over 3800 entries on application information, contact names, program descriptions and addresses for foundations that support individual artists. Scholarship, loan, and travel grant information are all included in this valuable, albeit expensive ($65), book.

The National Directory of Grantmaking Public Charities also has a section entitled "Grants to Individuals". This section highlights charities that give directly to individuals.

Jargon

An important issue with which you must be prepared to deal is arts jargon. Every profession has a secret language but no group has mastered jargon quite as skillfully as arts professionals. Arts administrators not only switch nouns with verbs (*impact* is a favorite multipurpose word) with impunity but create brand new words in each set of grant guidelines they design. New and non-words like *contextualization* are particularly popular these days.

In the early '90s, all artwork was required to *resonate*. If, in fact, your work did not *resonate* like a well-oiled vibrator, you simply had to kiss your chances for grant support good-bye. It was never up to you, of course, to judge the resonant qualities of your own work. The wise and godlike panel and foundation staff did that. All you could do was hope the video you'd submitted with your proposal was sending out warm vibrations to everyone assembled around the table.

After years as both a grant applicant and a grant panelist, my advice to the new applicant is this: Don't spend too much time trying to decipher hidden messages in the guidelines. It will screw you up and your chances of successfully figuring out what is in the mind of the guideline writers are very slim. Try to present your case honestly, use language most high school graduates can understand and pray there's someone on the panel like myself who will give bonus points for clarity. If you are persistent, you may reach a member of the staff who will actually spend time and try to clarify the mysteries of the guidelines for you.

It is also a mistake to try and match your mission to a particular set of guidelines. It almost never works. If your mission is to work with inner city kids to create documentary films, then you shouldn't change to fit some foundation's funding priority. In any event, the funding priority will change the next time the foundation's director or senior program officer changes and with luck, your work will be in style the next time the guidelines are rewritten.

If you are still Hell bent on participating in the sad and often humiliating grantsmanship game, there are a few other lessons to learn.

Although I had taken about a dozen grantsmanship classes and written more than fifty proposals prior to ever serving on a grants panel, my real education in the wonderful world of philanthropy came through the actual disbursal of grants. A couple of sessions on panels for the California Arts Council, the Brody Fund and the NEA taught me more about writing successful grant proposals than twenty years of on-the-job training. That experience also gave me great insight into what made my colleagues in the arts *resonate*. If either municipal or corporate funders invite you to participate on funding panels or even to bring coffee and rolls to other panelists they've selected, accept their offers. The experience will do you more good than a semester of classes in arts administration and grantsmanship.

I am now convinced some of the fifty proposals I wrote prior to becoming a grants panelist were actually funded because the law of averages and the gods were on my side. At the time, I mistakenly attributed my success to the quality of the organizations I represented and to the skills I assumed I had in preparing grant applications. I was, of course, quite naïve and dead wrong.

Most proposals that make it through the initial screening process at a foundation or government institution represent worthwhile organizations and are written competently.

Staff members usually weed out the unworthy and incompetent long before they make it to the desks of review panelists or Board members. The other elements which spell Life or Death for a grant proposal are far removed from issues of merit and competence and, sadly, influence funding outcomes far more than program quality and the writing skills of the applicant.

Good Old Boy/Girl Network

For example, nothing gives your grant application an edge like a connection to the Good Old Boy Network (which, in recent years, can also be the Good Old Girl Network). If you have even one champion on an eight person Board of Directors or grants panel, you're a good country mile ahead of your competitors. For many years, this accounted for the plethora of funding to large, mainstream arts institutions, to scientific research and to hospitals. Organizations serving minority populations or disciplines that were even slightly cutting edge ordinarily did not have staff and Board members who played golf with the CEOs of ARCO and Bank of America. Until recently, the decks were stacked and the playing field was not level. An application from a group of homeless minority artists had the proverbial snowball's chance in Hell of getting funding from 90% of the philanthropic foundations in the country.

Now that we are beginning to see a few independent women and minority men in Fortune 500 and Foundation Board Rooms, only about 80% of the philanthropic foundations in the country automatically reject applications from homeless minority artists. Who said "Speed kills"?

Fortunately, the homeless minority artists' opportunities for success are slightly higher when they apply to municipal funding agencies. No reasonably alert person will ever say their chances for success are good but they are certainly greater when they apply to private foundations. Since the Good Old Boy and Good Old Girl networks within government funding agencies are more often your peers (peers who are first among equals), the potential for a fair hearing increases significantly.

I don't know if they still do it but for many years, jaded grantsmanship trainers cautioned hopeful young development officers "it's all about who you know" and specialized in long "people give to people" lectures. They were not necessarily trying to discourage new and young fundraisers from entering the development field but were merely trying to clarify rules that unfortunately still prevail today.

Research

When you start down the onerous road to Grant Heaven, you should begin the journey with a lot of research. Find out the names of key foundation staff members and the names of the foundation's Board members. Depending on the size of your community, you may know some of these people or you may know someone who knows someone. In cities like Los Angeles and New York, actually getting an appointment with a person who has a key to the vault is very difficult but you should still at least try to make phone contact. Many foundation officers are more closely guarded than Saddam Hussein was after Desert Storm but even the least accessible staff members sometimes hold public meetings to discuss their funding guidelines. Try to attend these briefings before you invest time and money preparing a grant proposal for a foundation that has never funded your kind of program or organization.

As you become involved in researching the history and funding priorities of foundations and government agencies, you may discover the documentary film you plan to produce has already been made. You may also discover that the foundation from whom you hope to request funds has a long history of support for scientists engaged in the effort to wipe out acne but has not awarded a grant to an artist or arts organization in its twenty-five year history. On the up side, you may discover three foundations you never knew existed that fund exactly the kind of program you're designing. Be sure to check out the Bibliography and Resource Section for the names of books that will tell you more than you ever wanted to know about the priorities of corporate, foundation, and government donors.

At the risk of sounding too much like Sister Mary Margaret from Our Lady of Malibu Catholic School, I urge you to remember your manners when you talk to receptionists or assistants at each foundation office you contact. As basic as that advice sounds, I am still astonished, after many years of eavesdropping in the wonderful worlds of both business and government, when I hear callers rudely address people they perceive as powerless. The fact of the matter is, few people are as powerful at a foundation as a good secretary or administrative assistant who has been at the foundation for years. Not only do they know everything that is going on in their offices but they often give better advice and save you more time and effort than anyone else you will meet in the development business. The initial contacts you make within a funding agency may have a great bearing on whether you *ever* meet the agency's program officer or director.

It's strategically foolish to dismiss anyone because she or he does not have an impressive title. In addition to that, Sister Mary Margaret will document your conduct in the little diary she carries in her pocket. It's not worth the risk.

The point is, you will always need to have some direct human contact within a foundation or corporate funding arm or commission if you hope to have your proposal considered seriously. In an ideal world, one of your Board members will know one of the foundation's Board members and will have a chance to discuss the merits of your proposal over a cappuccino. In an almost ideal world, one of your Board members will know a program officer and will be able to call her about the proposal you've submitted. If you are very lucky, one of the panelists reviewing your grant application will be familiar with your organization and admire the work you're doing. If no one knows anyone and no one in the Western World has ever heard about your organization, you had better get to know the foundation receptionist and make sure he alerts you when public briefings on guidelines are being held. It may be the only chance you will have to introduce yourself and your program to the foundation's program officer.

Get to Know Your Colleagues

It is also important to get to know your colleagues in your field or discipline. Peer panelists chosen to evaluate grant applications at state arts councils, commissions or even to sit on panels for institutions such as The James Irvine Foundation or the California Community Foundation are selected for their knowledge and experience. Get to know as many people in your field as you can and make sure they know about your work or organization. If and when they are in a position to review your application, they will be able to speak from a position of knowledge.

If your organization is dependent on grant support, networking with your colleagues should be part of your job description. Keep them well informed about your programs, invite them for site visits, and send them copies of any press clippings about your successes. You may never be able to meet the Chairman of the Board at the Ahmanson Foundation but you can and should always meet your colleagues.

Reconcile your Narrative Statement With Your Financial Statement

Although I am convinced a well-written grant proposal is less important to outcome than connections within the funding agency, no one can get away with a proposal that is prepared sloppily or which has inconsistencies so egregious they offend even lawyers and hardened scam artists. If you cannot reconcile what you say in the Narrative portion of your proposal with your financial statement and budget, you'd better rethink and reword the Narrative. It's foolish to think you can get away with stating you served free lunches to 20,000 children in the preceding year if your financial statement indicates you only had enough money to fund meals for 5,000 children. If your statement on outreach to elderly citizens indicates you paid for a touring program to senior centers around the state, your budget should reflect fees for the artists who participated in the tour. Consistency in grant proposals is a major virtue.

Support Letters, Focus, and Thank You Notes

Support letters from the people you serve can strengthen a grant proposal. So do reviews, press clippings and an objective program evaluation. If you are fortunate enough to have hundreds of letters and press clippings in your files, be selective. Restraint is almost as important as consistency when it comes to preparing a grant request.

Every participant on a grants review panel has very personal preferences on what he or she likes to see included in the application package. I like to see evidence of program quality and others want to know that programs and services have reached thousands of constituents. I also like to see rhetoric held to a minimum. Anyone who tells me their organization is the *only*, the *best*, and the *most innovative* can lose me in the first paragraph. I like brief, focused statements which tell me in the first half-page the name of the applicant, who the applicant serves, and how much money they want. If you give me a Master's thesis to read, you've lost me and may not get me back. You have to remember that some grants panelists, particularly if they're working for state or federal arts councils, may have one or two hundred applications to read. You will never endear yourself or your organization to them by making them work too hard. Keep it short, keep it focused, keep it honest and let your support letters and reviews tell them if, indeed, you are the *only*, the *best*, and the *most innovative*.

When all is said and done and your proposal has been prepared, submitted, reviewed and rejected, spend a nano-second on self-pity and then <u>immediately</u> write Thank You notes to everyone who helped you with your grant application. This long list should include the foundation program officer who submitted your proposal to the panel, the foundation receptionist who took your twenty calls before you talked to the program officer, the people who wrote support letters for you and the staff members within your organization who prepared your budget, copied your press clippings and designed the program you attempted to fund.

Tenacity

If you can, find out why your request was rejected. Sometimes rejection has more to do with the foundation's priorities than the merits of your proposal. Sometimes there is something in your proposal that made a Board member or panelist anxious. If it's the latter, make your corrections and resubmit the proposal to another foundation or to the same foundation for their next deadline. As Winston Churchill said during World War II and Lance Armstrong said before the 1999 Tour De France, "Never, never, never give up." Tenacity apparently wins wars and long distance bicycle races. It certainly works in the strange and whimsical world of philanthropy.

Grant Proposal Outline

Most foundations and/or government funders will require the following in a request for funding:

Summary
Your summary should be the last part of the proposal you write and the first part of the proposal the funder reads. It should succinctly identify you or your organization, describe your project or program, and state the amount you are requesting from the foundation as well as the total cost of your project.

_____

_____

_____

_____

_____

_____

_____

_____

_____

_____

_____

_____

_____

_____

_____

_____

_____

Project Description

Use this space to clearly describe the what, how, when, where and why of your project. Describe who will benefit from your work and why it is significant. Be as realistic as possible and try to establish your program results in measurable terms. If 45 elderly artists will benefit from your theater workshops, say so. Be specific about staff requirements to implement your project, develop a timeline and discuss evaluation criteria.

_____

_____

_____

_____

_____

_____

_____

_____

_____

_____

_____

_____

_____

_____

_____

_____

_____

_____

_____

History of Organization

Describe your organization's history, its leadership, its major accomplishments, and its funding history.

_____
_____
_____
_____
_____
_____
_____
_____
_____
_____
_____
_____
_____
_____
_____
_____
_____
_____
_____
_____
_____

Board Endorsement

Enclose a letter signed by the Chair or an executive board member of your Board of Directors. The letter should indicate the project has the full support of the Board.

Financial Statements and Budget

If possible, include audited financial statements from the most recent fiscal year. Also enclose a current operating budget and a project budget.

Board Biographies and Staff Resumes

Include a Board list, resumes or bios of key Board members and resumes for project staff members.

Non-profit Documentation

Include a copy of your federal tax exemption letter (501 © 3 documentation).

Support Documentation

If relevant, enclose copies of reviews, press releases, support letters, selected programs, brochures and videos and tapes. Do not include every fan letter you ever received but provide enough support material to establish credibility. Also do not include tapes and videos of poor quality.

See the Bibliography and Resource Section for more information on grants funding.

SHOW ME THE MONEY!

A banker is a fellow who lends you his umbrella when the sun is shining and wants it back the minute it starts to rain.

Mark Twain

If you are a self-employed artist or woman business owner with a start up business, you are justified in assuming it is easier to win the Lottery than to get a bank loan. Banks have only actively marketed their services to women in the past ten years and their woman of choice is still a wealthy widow with more real estate than the Rockefellers. Unless your name is David Hockney or Placido Domingo, artists, for the most part, are viewed slightly less creditworthy than unemployed refugees with no collateral and poor cash flow.

Nonetheless, your prospects for finding money to support your art and/or business are not entirely hopeless. Almost every major bank now has a Women's Initiative that at least pays lip service to supporting women business owners. They all want to have women business owners they've supported to whom they can point proudly at the end of each year. You may as well be one of those women.

A number of foundations that offer grants and loans to individual artists are listed in the Resource Section at the end of the book.

This chapter will discuss loan criteria from conventional lenders as well as some alternative ways to finance your work.

The Five Cs To Credit

Although the five loan criteria bankers use to evaluate loan applicants is not unreasonable, few artists and women business owners manage to get a loan application approved. Many explanations are given for the failure to obtain investment capital. Some are valid, more are absurd. The fact of the matter is that banks, by choice and regulation, make low risk loans to established businesses. As a rule, neither artists nor women entrepreneurs have established businesses and more often than not, both are considered high risk. So before you waltz in to see your friendly neighborhood banker, put on the banker's hat and assess yourself against the following criteria:

Character counts. Your personal credit history and track record for paying personal bills and taxes is important. If you don't have a record of payments to mortgage companies and credit card companies but do have an exemplary record of timely rent and utility bill payments, present those to the loan officer. Tax liens are the kiss of death and if you have filed for bankruptcy in the past ten years, you probably won't get a loan until you have repaid your creditors.

Cash Flow is critical. If your new business has shown a profit for two or three years and if your net profit plus non-cash expenses equals $1.50 for each dollar of loan payments, your chances for loan approval are looking up. For sole proprietors, debt should be less than half your income.

Capital shows your commitment to your work and ideas. The amount of capital you invest in your own business is a reflection of your commitment and the strength of your company. Banks generally require a 30 to 35 percent cash infusion to offset what you are asking them to invest.

Collateral still counts. Although many banks now offer small uncollateralized loans, most small business loans are secured by cash reserves, real estate, inventory or equipment. These assets protect a lender in case of a sudden operational glitch.

Conditions and trends can provide a lender with a sense of security or anxiety about investing in another Beanie Babies venture or a new version of Pokemon. Bankers will want to know if you are in a growth industry and that your product is not hostage to a season or a fad that may die tomorrow. If you have the answer to the child care problem in America or an alternative, non-polluting energy source, your banker will look on you more kindly than if you are peddling nose rings and bell bottom trousers.

If, by your own assessment, you do not measure up to the five Cs, you should think about alternative funding sources such as microloans (see list of Microlenders in the Resource Section), factoring, bartering, credit card debt, and loans from friends and family.

ALTERNATIVE FINANCING

Loans from Friends and Family Members

Loans from friends and family members are one of the most common ways new businesses and growing businesses are financed. Of the $50 billion in "angel" capital that flowed to U.S. start up companies in 1997, more than $40 billion came from friends, rich uncles and other family members. In spite of this astonishing figure, I think borrowing from friends and family is one of the riskiest business transactions in which anyone can possibly engage.

Few relationships can survive the inevitable tension that occurs between a borrower and a lender. Payments are missed, expenses increase unexpectedly, inventory spoils or goes astray and the hundred crises no one anticipated *always* occur. In most instances, your grandmother does not lose her house and your brother's college tuition fund is replenished before he holds up a liquor store. Nonetheless, borrowing from friends and family causes stress that extends way beyond you and Uncle Moneybags.

This is my advice to family members tempted to acts of foolish generosity: Pretend you are making a gift rather than a loan. If you can cheerfully donate $10,000 to Cousin

Emily's new business and if you truly will not go crazy when you see her driving around town in a new sports car (long before she pays you back), then cash in your CDs and give Emily the money. If you know in advance you will be hurt, disappointed and angry when she fails to repay you, keep your CDs where they are.

If you persist in believing you can lend Emily your life savings and that she will be conscientious about repayment, draw up a contract outlining a payment schedule, a timeline for retiring her debt, and the amount of interest you expect to receive for the loan you make. Handle the transaction in as businesslike a fashion as you would if you were the neighborhood banker. Emily will still skip town and break your heart but a contract will at least set a tone and formally establish what your expectations are.

Always be philosophical about business arrangements with friends and family. If you lend someone $10,000 and never see them again, it is probably well worth it.

I also feel compelled to admonish the hopeful borrower: a loan from a close friend or family member may be low-interest but it is extremely high-risk. I have, on very rare occasions, survived the hazards of borrowing from friends but I do not recommend it for the faint of heart. You risk your friendship and your friend's friends will scorn you. Strained family relationships will extend far beyond the lender to cousins, aunts and in-laws. The lender's children will resent your cavalier attitude toward their inheritance. His parents will complain to your grandparents and your parents will be humiliated and forced to avoid all family gatherings for the rest of their natural lives.

Credit card debt, even at an exorbitant interest rate of 19%, may cost you much less in the long run than a no-interest loan from a close relative.

Credit Cards and Microloans

According to Arthur Anderson & Co., credit cards are now a source of financing for 34 percent of America's small businesses. In 1992 a study conducted by the National Foundation for Women Business Owners found that 52% of all women entrepreneurs used their credit cards for short-term financing. If you are disciplined enough to repay the money you "borrow" exactly as you would a conventional bank loan, credit cards with a low interest rate (below 10%) are actually an inexpensive option for financing a small business.

Microlending may be a better option. Microloan programs have been established by the SBA, by counties and by cities throughout the country. In addition, a list of over 400 members of the Association for Entrepreneurial Opportunity (AEO) can be found at the end of this book.

Generally, microloans are available in amounts ranging from $500 and $25,000. Some programs are low-interest, some are high-interest and some offer no-interest loans. Most do not require collateral and many are designed for borrowers who cannot qualify for conventional bank loans. Some microloan programs require applicants and borrowers to attend free or low-cost business training classes before loans are approved. This is very good news because few entrepreneurial 'wannabe's' have the business training they *always* need to make a success of their businesses.

Participating in a microloan program is a wonderful way to build a credit history. By the time you have repaid your microloan, you will have established a credit history you can literally "take to the bank" when you are ready for a larger, more conventional loan.

Participating in a microloan program can also provide you with a support system as well as the cash you need to start or grow your business. Technical assistance counselors and the mentors attached to microlending programs provide you with an early warning system to alert you to problems you might not, on your own, see coming.

If you have no or a flawed credit history, no collateral, and have been turned down by one or even two banks, microloans may be an appropriate option for you to explore. Check with your local SBA office or refer to the Resource Section for a list of microlenders in your state or county.

Bartering

Bartering is another option cash poor businesses frequently employ to cover items such as printing, shipping, accounting, maintenance, design work, and advertising. In its simplest form, bartering is the exchange of one company's products or services for those belonging to another company.

One company may exchange office space for computer services or trade office cleaning services for bookkeeping. It may be the one way you can afford to have a promotional brochure printed or to "pay" for the audit you need before you can apply for a large grant from a foundation. With over $7 billion in sales transacted each year by more than 300 barter exchanges in the commercial barter industry, bartering is obviously working for thousands of other American businesses.

On local or regional barter exchanges, you can offer company or personal products and services at market rate and swap them for goods provided by other exchange members. If the company with whom you are bartering can't use your services immediately, it can bank trade credits to be used later.

Barter Advantage, a New York barter exchange, publishes *Barter Basics*, a free booklet that describes different kinds of bartering arrangements. Call 212 534-7500 or 212 289-2900 and ask them to send information if you are seriously considering trading your company's services and products for another service or product. *Barter Basics* can also be reached by fax at 212 534-8145, 1751 2nd Avenue, Suite 103, New York, New York 10128. Their website address is www.barteradv.com.

You can also call the National Association of Trade Exchanges for the location of the barter exchange in your city or region. Their website is www.mutual.com/nate.

Factoring

Factoring is more expensive than other types of financing but companies that experience long delays in payment and lack the assets or collateral for bank financing sometimes use factoring as a financing option. For example, businesses that sell to government agencies often have to wait well beyond ninety days for payment. A factor will purchase your accounts receivable or purchase orders for between 50% and 90% of the amount your customers owe, give you the money immediately and give you the balance, minus administrative fees, once the customers pay up. Administrative fees vary depending on the quality and turnover of your receivables.

The Wall Street Journal reports that factoring firms financed over $75 billion in receivables in 1997 and that most of the financing went to small businesses.

If you think factoring may be a good business strategy for you, consult The Edwards Directory of American Factors, a publication developed by the Edwards Research Group at 800 963-1993.

Incubators

Although incubators generally do not help finance small businesses or individual artists, they can help you save a lot of money.

An incubator can provide a protective, favorable environment for your business during the start-up stage. Incubator spaces shared with other start-up businesses traditionally offer partially subsidized office and rehearsal space and the use of shared equipment such as faxes, copiers, computers, lighting/sound equipment, kilns, and editing equipment at a very low cost.

In addition to inexpensive rents, incubator businesses can share staff members, sell products and services to fellow incubator businesses, collaborate on performances and exhibitions, and receive development benefits such as training and education. They may also have access to low-cost legal and accounting services as well as voice mail, storage and post office boxes.

Incubators are not for everyone but their popularity is growing rapidly. In 1980 there were only 15 incubators in the country. By 1995 over 600 incubators belonged to the National Business Incubation Association (NBIA). Their popularity is doubtless driven by their success rate. Whereas only one in fifteen new businesses succeed, the success rate for businesses that start under the wing of an incubator is 80 percent.
Following the lead of arts incubators such as the one at the Colorado Center for Contemporary Arts and Crafts in Manitou Springs, artists and arts administrators are now exploring ways to establish incubator programs in states from California to New York.

For more information about incubator programs in your state, contact the National Business Incubation Association at 740 593-4331, fax 740 593-1996, www.nbia.org or write NBIA at 20 E. Circle Drive, Suite 190, Athens, Ohio 45701.

Bankers Want To Help. No, Really

Almost all major banks have seen the error of their ways and now have well-established and well-staffed Initiatives targeted specifically to the women's market. Our own Women Incorporated (WI) National Financial Network (NFN) has had a relationship with Bank One, BankBoston, The Money Store (recently merged with First Union) and many other conventional lending institutions for almost four years. To gain access to any of our NFN partners, loan applicants should call WI at 213 680-3375. We conduct a preliminary and relatively painless screening to determine the most appropriate lender for your business. If you need a standard SBA loan of $100,000 - $2 million, we will very likely refer you to The Money Store. If you are a small business owner in Massachusetts and want a $50,000 expansion loan, we might refer you to Teri Cavanagh, the Director of the Women Entrepreneurs Connection at BankBoston. Our goal is to get you a "Yes" the first time you apply for a loan and to make sure you don't waste your time with an institution unlikely to approve your request. For additional information about our National Financial Network, check our website at www.womeninc.com.

Other banks that have aggressively pursued the women's market in recent years include Wells Fargo, Bank of America, and Chase Manhattan. All have done business with either the National Association of Women Business Owners or with Women Incorporated. As their success with women entrepreneurs increases, so does their commitment. To paraphrase a veteran Civil Rights leader, "if you have them by the money belt, their hearts and minds will follow."

Creative Capital for Artists

Creative Capital, a new funding institution for artists, raised its hand in August, 1998, and began operations in January 1999. This national organization manages a revolving fund designed to support artists who pursue innovative, experimental approaches to content in the visual, performing and media arts.

In contrast to traditional charitable grants programs, Creative Capital will work closely with artists to help ensure the success of their projects by providing marketing and other non-artistic assistance that helps develop audiences for artists' work.

In return for Creative Capital's financial and managerial support, artists they support will share a portion of the proceeds generated by their projects with Creative Capital's Fund. The proceeds will replenish the $5 million fund and then support more artists in the future. The goal of Creative Capital is to raise $40 million and to support at least 60 individual artists annually over a period of twenty years.

For grant guidelines and additional information about Creative Capital, contact:

Ruby Lerner or Archibald Gillies
Creative Capital Foundation
C/o The Andy Warhol Foundation
65 Bleeker Street, 7th Floor
New York, New York 10012
212 598-9900
212 387-7555
Fax 212 598-4934
www.creative-capital.org

New Loan Programs From The SBA

In late 1998, the U.S. Small Business Administration (SBA) introduced two streamlined loan programs designed to provide more than $1 billion in hard-to-get loans for start ups, women and minority firms, and business owners in inner city and rural areas.

The programs, SBALowDoc and SBAExpress, target a gap in the marketplace for small business loans under $150,000. These programs make it easier and more attractive for lenders to make small SBA-backed loans and allegedly ensure a 36-hour turn-around on loan applications.

The SBA provides financial, technical and management assistance to help Americans start, run and grow their businesses. With a portfolio of business loans, loan guarantees and disaster loans worth more than $45 billion, the SBA is the nation's largest single backer of small businesses. Unfortunately, the SBA is something of a political football that is frequently under attack. Although it is the leading government agency to assist small business owners, there are often moves afoot to eliminate or weaken the agency. Depending on the political climate at any give moment, the SBA could lose much or all of its funding. It behooves women and all small business owners to stay informed about the political health and welfare of the U.S. Small Business Administration.

For more information about SBALowDoc and SBAExpress, check their web site at www. sba.gov/news/

Summing Up

Given the remarkable success rate of women business owners over the last few years, it is amazing how little support they have received from the country's financial institutions. The National Foundation for Women Business Owners (NFWBO) reports that the 9.1 million women business owners in the country now employ over 27.5 million people (far more than Fortune 500 companies employ worldwide) and generate over $3.6 trillion in sales annually. NFWBO's analysis shows that from 1987 to 1999, the number of women-owned firms in the U.S. increased 103%. Employment grew at a far more rapid rate of 320% and sales skyrocketed by 436%.

NFWBO also reports that women entrepreneurs continue to have less bank credit than do male business owners and that women of color face far greater difficulties in gaining access to capital. Colleen Anderson, Executive Vice President of Wells Fargo, the bank that sponsored the NFWBO study on access to capital and credit, said, "As the study indicates, there is still room for improvement and Wells Fargo is committed to lending qualified women business owners the $10 billion in our Women's Loan Program."

In other words, "We've come a long way, baby, but we've still got a long way to go."

HIRING, FIRING AND THE TIME WE SPEND IN BETWEEN

I'm better at firing than I am at hiring. Many of the people I've fired over the years are now close friends. One of the people to whom I dedicated this book often talks about the gift she bought me when I fired her from a position she had held for almost five years as the head of Costuming for a municipal theater department. Other people I've fired have taken me out to dinner and one even named her child after me. It is a small talent, I suppose, but firing well always beats firing badly.

Lunatics I've Hired

Hiring is another issue. Although I have a solid cadre of inspired employees with whom I have worked on multiple projects over a period of twenty years, I have also hired far more than my share of lunatics, slugs, criminals, incompetents and bad-asses. In no particular order, my Hit Parade includes

- A drug-addled actor who casually asked me for permission to kill his Director
- A bigamist whose wives both tried to attach his wages
- A transsexual who became too depressed to carry out her duties as a salesperson
- A secretary who spent the first thirty minutes of every incoming call describing her chaotic love life to my clients
- A former felon who convinced me his arrest for grand theft auto should be no deterrent to his dream of becoming a museum guard
- A file clerk who filed client records according to some mysterious code related to the freeway system in Southern California
- A special events coordinator who, unbeknownst to me, had sued every previous employer she'd ever had, and
- An executive assistant who "borrowed" my car for three weeks to visit her boyfriend in San Diego and mysteriously returned it to me *sans* stereo and hubcaps.

I have hired people with chips on their shoulders, multiple personalities, immigration problems, and an amazing lack of usable skills. Given my astonishing inability to read a person's character, it is probably not surprising that I developed a real flair for firing. Practice makes perfect.

I have learned to compensate for my deplorable inability to hire wisely by having other people do it for me. I don't hire anyone anymore. Secretaries, executive assistants, bookkeepers, financial consultants, and especially baby-sitters are all hired by other people who know me, understand the job that needs to be filled, and don't have to be hit between the eyes with a two by four to recognize a nut case or a scam artist.

If you feel you're a good judge of character and can hire competent, honest people, you should still be conscientious about checking references. Although employers concerned about lawsuits may be gun shy about divulging too much about former employees, you can pick up a lot from a tone of voice or if someone hesitates before answering. Try asking questions that require more than a one-word answer such as: Why did Jane leave her job? Why would you rehire her? What did her colleagues think about her? When checking references, learn to assess both what is not said as well as what is said.

When you interview the job applicant, be sure you ask questions that give you a real sense of the person sitting in front of you. Asking the applicant to describe her employment history will give you a sense of the environment in which she is comfortable as well as her tolerance for risk. Small, entrepreneurial and start-up companies need to be wary of someone who has been employed for years by a Fortune 500 company. Chances are, the applicant did not linger in the corporate world by mistake. The security and the culture of the corporate world are a couple of planets away from the small start up. Business owners are frequently flattered when obviously competent corporate executives show interest in working for their small businesses. However, hitting your head on the glass ceiling does not necessarily prepare you for a position of responsibility in a fly-by-the-seat-of-your-pants business. More often than not, the corporate refugee will begin to miss the benefits, the protocol, and the security of the Fortune 500 company within six months.

"What is your biggest mistake?" is another good question to ask a job applicant. If the applicant sidesteps the question with a reference to some trivial mishap, press her further. If she describes a major problem she helped create and appears to have learned from the experience, she may be exactly the kind of person you want in your company. People who are accountable, take responsibility and can "own" their shortcomings are more valuable than people who appear perfect but who specialize in passing the blame on to others.

Although the final decision is yours, it's a good idea to have more than one person at your company participate in interviewing candidates for a job. Different people will have different insights and will see qualities and strengths in the candidate you may miss. In addition, you will be able to observe how others in your company are likely to react to someone you may add to the company team. At minimum, other people you involve in the hiring process will feel invested in the new employee when she comes aboard and will help ease her into the fabric of your company.

An opportunity to interview with several people in a company will also give a job applicant a sense of the "company culture" in which she'll be working. She will be able to assess how existing employees interact with one another before she makes a long-term commitment to work for your company.

Firing Friends, Firing Felons

As bad as I am at hiring, I am *that* good at firing. Providing I do it alone and follow my instincts to handle the dismissal in a natural and compassionate way. It also helps if I have not been previously traumatized by a lecture from a Human Resources officer on the fate that awaits me if I use one wrong word or smile inadvertently. In tandem with someone else or following the Human Resources lecture, I handle firing just as miserably as 99% of other employers who take on this thankless job. Left to my own resources, 90% of the time I can end a working relationship without a law suit, the filing of a grievance or even anger.

Unless you are dealing with people totally out of touch with reality, a dismissal rarely comes as a surprise to the person on the firing line. In the best of all possible worlds, there is a paper trail with honest performance appraisals outlining areas in which the employee falls short. If an employee has been given an opportunity to improve or correct his performance and has not done so, he will be more painfully aware of this than anyone else.

Most of the time, an employee who doesn't make it has fallen afoul of The Peter Principal and has been hired or promoted to a position for which he is ill suited. If an employee is hired for the wrong position (a grand theft auto felon is probably not the best choice for a museum guard position), the manager is far more to blame for the employee's "failure" than anyone else. Very good engineers and excellent technicians often make terrible managers when they're promoted. Great teachers are not always good principals. Brilliant artists are seldom creative and competent administrators. If we don't hire wisely and don't give our employees the tools they need to succeed, then we can hardly blame them when they come up short.

My success as a firing machine comes from my willingness to acknowledge my own shortcomings as a trainer, and as a supervisor in matching the employee to the job. I have never tried to make anyone feel like a personal failure for a professional shortcoming and when I can honestly do so, I try to recommend the person I'm dismissing for a job that *is* appropriate. If the person is honest and has a good attitude, I try very hard to make the dismissal as painless and humane as possible.

When I fired my good friend as the Costumer for the theater company, I had no problem recommending her for other costuming jobs. I fired her simply because we were producing contemporary plays and were no longer doing Period or Children's Theater productions that required costumes. Although she was a model employee and an excellent Costumer, changes within her department meant that her job had been eliminated. I toyed with the idea of moving her into an administrative position but she and I both realized a great Costumer does not (necessarily) a great Administrator make. It was far better to give her glowing reference letters, help her with her job search, and keep her as a friend rather than to force her into a position that would never fit.

When one is faced with the necessity to fire nut cases and people who think they should be in charge of the Universe, all bets are, of course, off. People who are dishonest, destructive, and/or undisciplined in a variety of interesting ways should be dismissed as fast as you can do the paperwork. If you can't trust an employee, you shouldn't keep him or her around a nano-second longer than it takes to cover your ass with documentation. There's no point in giving them notice or time to put poison in the office water cooler, and you sure as hell don't want to recommend them for another job.

I have learned to my sorrow that keeping a bad apple around because you think they'll reform or because you hope there will be a better time in the future to fire them is the Grandmother of Bad Ideas. There is never a better time to fire a bad apple or a nut case than NOW. Do it fast, do it clean and do it unemotionally. Everything I said about dismissing someone in a compassionate, humane and gracious fashion applies only to honest and decent people who, often through no fault of their own, have ended up in the wrong job. People who are delusional or evil don't get reference letters and going away parties, and even guilt-ridden former Catholic girls do not dedicate books to them.

In large companies, managers too often "pass the buck" and give an inadequate employee an adequate or even good evaluation knowing the employee will be promoted or passed on to another department. The sad side of this is that the employee often does not know he is inadequate. Until some manager with *huevos* finally bites the bullet and presents the employee with an objective performance appraisal, he has every reason to believe the company is satisfied with his performance. He has, after all, been told repeatedly that his work is satisfactory.

When the new manager confronts the employee with a different assessment, he must do it in such a way that protects himself as well as the company. In this litigious day and age, employers must be aware of the concept of personal liability in employment issues. It is extremely difficult to give someone a critical evaluation after they've been receiving complimentary evaluations for years. Everyone's life is easier and the company is far less vulnerable if, from day one, you make a commitment to do honest and objective performance appraisals. Ultimately, this kind of straightforward approach also works to the benefit of the employee.

In small companies, a supervisor tends not to take the easy way out because he knows the problem employee will continue to be his problem. As an employer with one or two employees, it is very much to your advantage to do regular and honest performance appraisals. Managing even a few employees is extremely labor-intensive but it is critical to the success of your business that you do it and do it well. Artists with home-based businesses or small companies and studios are no exception to this rule. You'll spend far more time away from your art re-doing everything you've mismanaged than you will if you learn to manage your employees correctly from the moment they're hired.

Hiring Contractors

Some employers try to circumvent management issues by hiring contractors. For example, if you have payroll responsibilities, you can outsource work to a payroll service. This not only reduces your headcount and headaches, but enables you to concentrate on other tasks that add value to your business.

You may be courting trouble if you try to pass your secretary off as an independent contractor. While you may avoid paying him benefits, you will still have the same management and supervisory responsibilities and you will also have the IRS on your tail before you can spell p-r-i-s-o-n. The IRS has a long checklist to determine whether or not someone passes the test as an independent contractor but if a contract employee is

- Supervised by you
- Doing work you assign
- Spends most of his time housed in your office and
- Has no other clients,

you probably should invite him to the annual Employee Picnic. You should also save up for the fine you're going to pay the IRS for trying to pass off an employee as an independent contractor.

Bill What-A-Guy Gates is legendary for a lot of reasons, not the least of which is hiring contractors who couldn't pass the IRS Sniff Test at a Skunk Convention in July. How does he get away with it? Basically, he has the money to fight the government in court for as long as he wants to. By the time the issue is settled, even if he pays a fine, the cost to him will be insignificant compared to the money he made while he was putting the government lawyers through their paces. As a slightly cynical twenty-year Human Resources veteran observed, "Money talks, bullshit walks, and the rich get richer."

Assuming you have fewer resources with which to taunt the IRS than Mr. Gates, you should err on the side of caution with contractors. Outsourcing to companies with other clients for services such as payroll, public relations, accounting, and legal services is safe and may be cost effective. On the other hand, full-time technical directors, secretaries, or receptionists with no other clients will get you in a lot of trouble if you try to pass them off as contractors.

There are a number of excellent books that address hiring and firing as well as other management issues. The Chamber of Commerce usually offers their members free publications about employee relations, labor laws, and grievance procedures. Tom Peters has written a number of books on management and leadership, including *In Search of Excellence* and *Thriving On Chaos.* Mary Jane Parson focuses on problems small business owners' face in her book, *Managing the One-Person Business.* Women Incorporated's *The Busy Woman's Guide To Successful Self-Employment,* written by Dr. Marsha Firestone and Bernard Fortunoff, also has a chapter entitled "Hiring Well and Managing With Ease" that includes several useful management assessment tools for the new employer or manager.

NOTES

PLANNING

My friend, Hope Tschopik Schneider, changed my Karma one year when we were travelling between Kathmandu and Pokhara. She's that kind of woman. The Fates bend to her will.

She is also the best planner I know. In 1984, when she was the associate director and vice president of the Olympic Arts Festival, she left nothing to chance and it showed. The Festival was a glorious celebration of the arts. Set on stages throughout Los Angeles, artists from countries all over the world arrived on time, performed exquisitely and left town without incident with bankable paychecks. Credit for this had to be shared but the largest bundle of bouquets should have been laid at Hope's doorstep.

By contrast, in 1990, when I assumed Hope's position at the Los Angeles Festival, life was a tad more chaotic. Neither Peter Sellars, the Festival's brilliant artistic director, nor I was known for exemplary planning skills. While we still presented thousands of inspired artists on seventy-one stages throughout Los Angeles and while most of the artists arrived on time and performed exquisitely, there were *many* incidents before the last artist left town.

Actually, some of those artists are still in town.

Our festival was known for its free-flowing joy and for the efforts we made to infiltrate every barrio and ghetto in Los Angeles. It was also known for

- a record number of defectors (Cambodia and China)
- artists from New Zealand who spontaneously decided to disappear from the Artists' Village at UCLA in order to visit a Hopi reservation in Arizona before heading home
- throat singers who left the Festival early to catch the big hunt back home at Eskimo Point and
- large numbers of indigenous dancers who were lost in the Mexico City airport en route from the jungle to LAX.

Clearly Peter's and my approach to planning was different from Hope's.

In the decade between "our" Festival and now, I have seen the error of my ways and have come to realize that planning does not necessarily prohibit spontaneity and joy. To the contrary, sensible planning actually can provide an environment in which spontaneity and joy flourish. That's what Hope does. She provides an environment in which fabulous activity can occur without fear that lights will be turned off, offices will be padlocked and the staff will finish the work week only to discover the bank account housing their salaries has been attached by the IRS.

Her comments in the following article not only reflect my (current) views on planning but should become required reading for anyone running a small business or a non-profit arts organization.

Planning: Plain and Simple By Hope Tschopik Schneider

"To be uncertain is uncomfortable, but to be certain is ridiculous." – Chinese Proverb

As a veteran consultant to both the Advancement Grant Program and the Challenge Grant Program of the National Endowment for the Arts, I have come to the conclusion that most organizations do not have to engage in elaborate planning processes to be high-performance organizations. There is a place for the long-range plan, the multi-year plan, the strategic plan or whatever other name you want to call it, but the cost of doing these kinds of plans far exceeds the benefit under the normal operating conditions most organizations face.

There are three reasons to allocate the time and resources to develop these elaborate planning documents. Otherwise, planning, plain and simple, will do just fine. These three conditions are:

- The environment in which an organization exists changes dramatically when there are dramatic and sudden cut-backs in corporate, foundation or government support or when there are clear signals that the organization is losing its audience and/or its individual patrons.
- An organization is operating at capacity and a potential for growth exists, such as when a theatre contemplates moving from a 99-seat house to a larger theatre or a museum contemplates adding more exhibition space. In some instances, the addition of a new program or area requires a more comprehensive approach to planning.
- An organization undergoes a change in leadership after a long period of stable leadership and the mission of the organization needs to be reviewed, updated and reconfirmed by all stakeholders.

In any of these scenarios, it is worth the time and effort to hire a planning consultant to facilitate and manage a planning process in order to keep it neutral, open, honest and, perhaps most important, moving along.

Otherwise, planning is an on-going organizational function that need not be elaborate nor entail endless meetings with reams of paper. Planning, plain and simple, is a bit like a prescription for good health. Just like eating a balanced diet, getting regular exercise and flossing your teeth, planning is a good habit to develop. Some people think about planning as a road map, or a statement of goals and objectives, or a calendar with a To Do list. It is certainly all of these things. But in the final analysis, planning is just a series of ever-repeating questions or, in brief, an organizational mantra.

Planning at its most essential level performs the coordinating brain function in a complex system. An organization can be thought as nothing more than a human system which coordinates activity so that something happens. These activities fall neatly into functional areas:

- programming (what we are doing)
- marketing (how we are communicating outside the organization about what we are doing to attract business)
- development (how we are raising support, both human and financial)
- financial (how we track and report revenue and expenses)
- executive (how we coordinate all this activity and stay on mission).

Each one of these areas has its own plan of action, which details what action is taken, when and by whom. In many organizations, these operational plans are tacit and informal. Organizations with continuity of staff and leadership often follow a plan, which has been thoroughly established and is well worn. Everyone knows what to do in March or any other month of the year without referring to anything or having a meeting about it. In these organizations planning is simultaneous with actions and almost synonymous to the annual budgeting cycle when all these operational plans get reduced to numbers and pulled together into one document. This is a process which is cryptic, tacit, allows for gigantic loopholes in a structure of accountability and keeps decision-making masked and hidden.

Given this is a prevalent reality, an organization that wants to improve its planning can do so, easily and readily, by making explicit this on-going informal process and turning it into an explicit, fully engaged and engaging, thoughtful process. To do this, planning and evaluation need to happen simultaneously. Planning becomes about posing the right questions to every member of the organization and not about daily doing and periodically creating the lengthy wish list with an inflated budget to go with it. Planning also becomes endless. There is no real beginning or end because the questions are on-going and the search for answers, information, and data is updated on a daily basis.

Planning, plain and simple, in keeping with its name, begins at the beginning.

Where Are We?

Many of my clients have gotten into real trouble because they know more about where they want to go than where they are. Or to rephrase, they have more of an acquaintance with how they want to be than who they actually are. Self-knowledge, or knowing where you are, can be brutal and frightening. It is a landscape where the word "should" has no meaning. It is a reality which understands that an organization has no control of the external environment. It can only try to understand the environment accurately, and through self-knowledge, try to exert some influence upon it.

This means that planning starts with these questions.

- What do we do?
- Who cares? (Who is our audience? Demographics. Who are our sustaining patrons? Demographics.)
- What is it that they care about? (How do they perceive and evaluate our offerings? Are there differences by sub-groups?)
- How many care? (How wide is our base of support and interest?)
- How loyal is our audience? (Subscribers vs. Single Ticket Buyers-number, numbers,
- Renewal rate)
- How does this year's audience compare to last? (Trends over time change.)
- Who is our competition?
- What is distinctive about what we do versus our competition? (Qualitative assessment)
- How do we compare? Really!!!

If this sounds like basic market research, it is. The word to stress in the previous sentence is <u>basic</u>, as in fundamental, as in essential, as in minimal requirement for doing business. PERIOD. Every organization needs to be able to answer these questions well and accurately on an on-going basis. The minute there is a shift in the fundamental responses, the organization needs to prepare for a possible change in course. Go directly to strategic planning!

Where Do We Want To Go?

Other clients have had serious problems because they lost track of the mission in pursuit of the market. Envisioning is of primary importance to any arts organization; our business is creativity. We do have a mandate to lead and a caveat to not simply follow the market.

- What do we do?
- How do our activities serve as living examples of our mission?
- What is our impact? Are we confusing activity with impact? (Qualitative assessment)
- Do we need to change? (More, less, different?)
- Does our mission need to change? (Yes, go directly to strategic planning!)
- What does success look like? (I like this question a lot. It helps formulate "objectives" because it requires <u>concrete</u> answers).

How Much Is It Going To Cost?

A common mistake is underestimating the cost, either in human resources or financial resources, of doing business.

- What is it going to take to do programming, manage, market, fundraise, maintain the physical plant and evaluate operations? (Prepare a thorough costing of every functional area based on activity level, human productivity estimations and cost estimations)

- What are the budget assumptions? State them clearly, up front, in black and white. (Evaluate the underlying assumptions on direct costs and make explicit assumptions about human productivity)
- When do we need the money? When do we usually receive the money? (Cash flow is a critical financial dynamic to understand)
- What are our financial ratios and are they changing? (% Earned: Total Expenditures; Earned: Contributed; % of various categories of support to total support; the quick ratio-liquid assets: accounts payable. How do these compare from year to year? What are the trends?)
- Are we in debt? (yes, go directly to strategic planning!)

Where's The Money?

The fundamental demand for services in aggregate and on average in the arts has not changed wildly from year to year. (Some say there's been a steady decline because of declining government support.) The macro trend is not necessarily the micro trend. There are clear trends of decline or increase for individual organizations or differing geographic locales that can be discerned over time but the point is that most changes are gradual and incremental, whether you are evaluating contributed or earned revenues. Nevertheless, it is not uncommon for a professional planner to see a first draft of a client's budget which posits modest increase in expenses (i.e. business as usual or a little bit "more") and dramatic increases in revenue (usually to balance an unbalanced budget. Understandable but not acceptable). History has taught us that this scenario is not plausible. Dramatic increases in revenue require dramatic change in organizational behavior, organizational expenditure and/or environment, all of which suggest: Go directly to strategic planning!

- Who cares? Research, research, research.
- What do they value?
- How do they get their information?
- What elements of "service" are important to them?
- How do we best communicate with them? (What are the elements and sequencing of the marketing plan?)
- How much will it cost to communicate with them?
- Are we effective in our communications? Are we putting out scarce resources to the highest and best use? (Cost/benefit analysis; response rate; productivity analysis)
- Are the purchasing habits of our audience changing? Are we developing new tools?
- Are we developing and replenishing our audience? How? Evaluation?

A variation of all these questions can be created for the development function.

How Do We Pull All This Information Together?

Planning and evaluation go hand in hand. The process is reiterative and cyclical. All organizations think and organize themselves differently and there is no one correct way to create a planning/evaluation cycle. The simplest cycle I have observed is an organization on a July 1 to June 30 fiscal year. Its planning horizon is one-and-a- half years. (Some organizations need to think out three years because of the need to make contractual commitments. Three years need be no more complex than one-year planning horizons; the process of inquiry is the same). It is a mature organization in a stable environment. Most of its revenues are earned. The planning and evaluation function is conducted as a board purview with support from staff vetted through committees. The board meets on a bi-monthly basis. There is no planning committee per se but a planning/evaluation function is integrated into every meeting as an agenda item. The treasurer provides a Year to Date Report with variance analysis against budget at every board meeting.

MONTH	PLAN - EVALUATION
May	Board retreat. Evaluation of year's performance to date in all areas. Goal setting for the year, review of program – instruction to staff to develop programmatic objectives and work plan to support goals.
July	Review of final numbers in functional areas, discussion of trends: marketing, development. Program plan refinements presented by staff for discussion.
September	Review and approval of the annual audit. Discussion of long-term financial trends.
November	Preliminary discussion on marketing and development issues particularly in the area of pricing and market demand trends (changes in customer base, competition). Review of marketing and development strategy and assessment of tactical productivity overtime.
January	First draft of Budget prepared for board review.
March	Budget approved.
May	It begins again. Planning: plain and simple.

BUSINESS PLANS

Now that you've absorbed everything Hope has to say about Planning, I will provide you with a Business Plan Outline, Plain and Simple. Although I can name a dozen millionaires I've met personally who never wrote Business Plans, I can also name a hundred entrepreneurs whose business plans guided them to their positions of success.

I also recognize that five-or even three-year financial projections in this age of cyberspace are a joke but if you don't have them, bankers and investors will toss your loan applications in the circular file so fast your head will spin.

Think of your projections as a mechanism for measuring your progress and for keeping in touch with reality. Almost everyone who prepares a Business Plan for the first time inflates profits and underestimates both expenses and the time it will take to get a business up and running. Consequently, new business owners are invariably shocked when they discover the projections they had considered conservative are at least 200% too optimistic. Reality bites.

Preparing a Business Plan really is a great deal like preparing a proposal for a major grant. Both begin with an Executive Summary and end with Financial Documentation. In between these two sections you describe your business or project, talk about your management team, your marketing plan and your plan for success. If you've done one, you can manage the other. The main difference between arts organizations applying for grants and small businesses looking for growth capital is that arts organizations must write a grant request if they want a grant. Businesses don't necessarily have to prepare a business plan (although they should) if they're looking to friends and family for their investment capital.

While most Business Plan Outlines are alike, completed plans vary in size, depth and substance. Businesses in search of $100 million in investment capital will require a weightier document than a start-up business looking for $25,000. The $100 million business plan will actually cost more than $25,000 to prepare. The following outline is definitely NOT meant to satisfy the multi-million dollar investor. Rather it is meant to serve the needs of a start-up business owner or an entrepreneur looking to expand a small business.

Business Plan Outline

FIRST IMPRESSIONS
2708 East Ocean Boulevard
Long Beach, California 90802
Phone 562 XXX-XXXX
Fax 562 XXX-XXXX
Email address: firstimp@aol.com

Principals:

Janet Trondle
Antonio Banderas

This business plan is confidential. The reader is asked to respect its confidentiality and to return it to First Impressions.

Table of Contents

Pages should be numbered and each major section should begin on a new page.

TABLE OF CONTENTS

Executive Summary

The Executive Summary introduces your business to a lender or investor. Start with your mission statement, prepare a brief, concise overview of your business and summarize, briefly, each of the major sections of your plan. When the reader finishes the Executive Summary, she should understand a little bit about your business, your target market, your management team, and your company's financial goals and objectives for at least a three-year period.

Mission Statement

_____

_____

_____

_____

Overview of Business

Background

_____

Economic Climate

_____

Trends

_____

Target Market

_____

Management Team

_____

Company Financial Goals and Objectives

_____

_____

Business or Product Description

This section provides a more detailed description of your product or service and discusses, at length, what distinguishes your company from your competition. You should describe the life cycle of your product as well as growth opportunities for your company. Describe your target markets by age, gender, income, and geography. Explain why these customers will buy and continue to buy your product or service.

Life Cycle of your Product

_____

_____

_____

Growth Opportunities

_____

_____

_____

Target Market (full profile of consumer)

_____

_____

_____

Rationale for sales

_____

_____

_____

_____

Operations

You have an opportunity in this section to describe how you will run your company, who your suppliers are, how you will handle inventory, quality control, and the capital expenditures you will need to make to make your business a success.

Management Philosophy and Structure

_____

_____

_____

Vendors and Suppliers

_____

_____

_____

Inventory

_____

_____

_____

Quality Control

_____

_____

_____

Capital Expenditures

_____

_____

_____

Management

Describe your legal and management structure, consultants with whom you work, and anyone else you will call on to help you build and manage your business. Special emphasis should be placed on your CEO, CFO, accountant, and attorney. Include an Organization Chart in this section. If you are running a non-profit organization or a company that has a Board of Directors, include information about the background of each director.

Management Structure

_____

_____

Legal Structure (are you a partnership, a non-profit business, a sole proprietorship?)

_____

_____

Consultants

_____

_____

Management Team

_____

_____

Attachments

_____

_____

Organization Chart

_____

_____

Board of Directors (biographical information)

_____

_____

Market Research

This is your chance to show your stuff and demonstrate you know more about your market than anyone else. Describe the size of your market, the location of your primary and secondary customers, your competition, the unique features of your product or service, your rationale for pricing, your product testing and focus groups, and the resources you utilized to analyze your market.

Market Size

_____

_____

Location of Primary Customers

_____

_____

Location of Secondary Customers

_____

_____

Profile of Competition

_____

_____

Unique Features of Product or Service

_____

_____

Rationale for Pricing

_____

_____

Description of Focus Groups and Product Tests

_____

_____

Resources

_____

Marketing Plan

Read the Marketing Plan chapter.

Promotions

Read the Promotions chapter.

Financial Information

If you are not an accountant and can't afford to hire one to help with this part of your business plan, you're in a lot of trouble. You can try to find Accountants for the Public Interest on the Internet or you can try to trade a service or samples of your product for the services of an accountant (see Resource Section). Whatever you do, do not turn your business plan over to a loan officer without having an accountant review what you write and the information you provide in this section of your plan.

To begin, even if it's pathetic, <u>summarize your current financial status</u>. Where do you currently get your money and what have you put aside for operations and growth? How much working capital do you have and how will you use it (month by month) over a period of two years? How much money do you need to borrow, where will it come from and how will you repay it?

You will need a <u>Statement of Profit and Loss</u> for the last three years you've been in business. If you are starting a new business, you will need three years of <u>Projections</u>. To determine your Profit or Loss, subtract your Expenses from your Revenues or Income. Remember, this is the time to let every conservative bone in your body take over. Loan officers tend to be impatient with Pie in the Sky plans because they're asked to swallow so many of them.

When you estimate your sales (monthly over a three-year period), estimate low. When you project expenses, include everything from fixed costs such as rent, business taxes, and salaries to variable costs such as shipping and handling, design, and research. Expenses should also be projected month by month for at least a three-year period.

Your Business Plan should include a monthly <u>Cash Flow Statement</u> for one year and quarterly cash flow projections for years two and three. While your cash flow projections must show you have enough money to pay your bills and stay in business, this is another section where your conservative genes should kick in.

The following Cash Flow chart was designed by Dr. Marsha Firestone and Bernard Fortunoff for *The Busy Woman's Guide to Successful Self-Employment*, the book they created for Women Incorporated.

CASH FLOW
Year One – Hasty Hearth

	Jan	Feb	Mar	Apr	May	Jun	Jul	Aug	Sep	Oct	Nov	Dec
Cash in Bank 1st day of Month	$20,000	6,967	9,594	12,164	14,466	13,533	16,350	14,817	12,829	12,104	11,829	10,994
Expected Sales (Subscription at $15)	$3,000	6,000	6,000	4,500	4,500	4,500	4,500	4,500	6,000	6,000	6,000	9,000
Total cash receipts	$23,000	12,967	15,594	18,164	18,966	20,033	20,850	19,317	18,829	18,104	17,829	19,994
Less Expenses	$16,033	3,373	3,430	3,698	3.433	3,683	6,033	6,488	6,725	6,275	6,835	5,920
Cash Balance at end of month	$6,967	9,594	12,164	14,466	15,533	16,350	14,817	12,829	12,104	11,829	10,994	14,074

ASSUMPTIONS:

1. Equipment, furniture and renovations paid for in the first month.
2. Staffing would be $300 for the first six month; $600 for the second six months.
3. Supplies (food, etc.) would average $5,000 a year.
4. Operations (phones, electricity, office supplies, etc.) would average $4,000 a year.
5. The marketing budget for the year was $8,000.
6. The printing budget for the year was $20,000.
7. Average cost of mailing a newsletter each month – 15 cents.
8. Vandervort and Jordonsky would begin taking salaries in the seventh month. Vandervort would get $1,000 a month and Jordonsky would get $500.

Following this Cash Flow Statement, calculate your Break-even Point by determining when your gross profits equal your total expenses.

Increase Revenue or Reduce Expenses

Small businesses create over $3.6 trillion a year in Gross National Product, yet only one in fifteen new small businesses succeed. Why such a high fatality rate? There is no mystery about money. Cash flows out when you pay the cost to operate a business. Cash flows in when the client pays for your product or service. What's the problem?

If you need more money, why not increase the number of sales made? (Especially if your "painted seashell" inventory has reached the maximum storage capacity in your existing "rented" facility). You could decrease your prices and hope the volume of sales will offset the lower price per item. But what happens if you hit a slump in sales? Decrease the price a second time? You could increase the price of the service you perform. However, if you do, you could lose some of your existing clients. Customer loss might negate any profits you might have made from the increase.

This is an issue both entrepreneurs and major corporations face on a daily basis. For those of you who have MBAs from those good business schools, skip to the next chapter. For everyone else out there who buys the first appealing items they see in the front rows of the grocery store (even though there is a less expensive product one aisle away), read on. What you are about to learn is a simplified approach to the concept of business finance.

Cost of doing business

Business costs can be broken down into two categories: fixed costs (FC) and variable costs (VC). Fixed costs are costs that do not change with production. Variable costs are costs that do change, especially with production.

The following chart has a few examples of typical business costs.

FIXED COSTS (FC)	VARIABLE COSTS (VC)
Administration	Interest*
Depreciation	Materials
Interest*	Repairs/Maintenance
Property Taxes	Selling Expenses
Rent	Supplies
Utilities*	Utilities*
*FC/VC	*FC/VC

(In the long run, fixed costs may become variable if/when they change. For example, rent can go up).

When your product or service is sold for a price, the objective is to cover the fixed and variable costs. The remaining money from selling after these costs are covered is margin or profit. One sure way to make more profit or margin is to decrease fixed and/or variable costs. For example, you might reduce your fixed costs by:

- ꓱ Replacing the $2,000 rent for your studio with a $500 mortgage payment.
- ꓱ Spreading your total fixed costs by producing more "seashells". This creates more margin by reducing the fixed cost each "seashell" has to cover. For example:

If the total fixed cost = $2.50

1 Seashell produced	FC=$2.50
2 Seashells produced	FC=$1.25
5 Seashells produced	FC=$ .50

- ꓱ If you pay for a display space in a gallery or retail store, negotiate a higher commission rate on goods sold instead of a fixed monthly rate.

Breaking Even

Break-even has to do with the amount of sales necessary for a product or project to recover all associated "costs." In other words, the break-even point is reached when total revenue or income equals "fixed" plus "variable" costs. Theoretically, you can run a break-even business forever since all costs are covered. However, your goal should be not to break-even but to make a profit as soon as possible.

Returning once again to our "Seashells By The Seashore" analogy, I arbitrarily determine fixed costs to be $765.00. The seashell variable cost is $3.00 and I have decided I will sell each shell for $7.50. Following are two examples on how to figure my break-even point.

Example #1

A basic formula in figuring break-even is to subtract your variable costs from the selling price of your product. This sum would then be divided into your total fixed costs. Using this method to figure break-even, I would need to sell 170 seashells before I can realize a profit. The chart on the next page further illustrates this formula.

Fixed Costs (FC)	$765.00
Selling Price – Cost of Goods Sold (VC)	($7.50-$3.00)
	$765.00
	$4.50
Number of products sold in order to break-even	170 seashells
$ break-even	170 seashells x $4.50=$765.00

Example #2

I've re-evaluated my fixed and variable costs and decided on a fair price for each seashell. In this example I'm using a fixed cost of $500.00, a variable cost of $2.50, and a $5.00 price tag for each seashell.

Quantity Sold	Price per shell	Total Revenue	Variable Cost (VC)	Total Variable Cost	Fixed Cost (FC)	Total Cost	Profit
0	$5.00	0	$2.50	0	$500.00	$500.00	-$500.00
50	$5.00	$225.00	$2.50	$125.00	$500.00	$625.00	-$400.00
100	$5.00	$500.00	$2.50	$250.00	$500.00	$750.00	-$250.00
200	$5.00	$1,000.00	$2.50	$500.00	$500.00	$1,000.00	0
250	$5.00	$1,250.00	$2.50	$625.00	$500.00	$1,125.00	$125.00
300	$5.00	$1,500.00	$2.50	$750.00	$500.00	$1,250.00	$250.00

My break-even point was at $1,000.00 in sales and 200 seashells in products sold. Using this chart I can see when my business begins to show a profit and how the profit increases with the number of "seashells" sold.

(Note: _An increase or decrease in the price per shell will move the break-even point. Anytime costs are changed, break-even and margin/profit should be recalculated_).

Conclusion

Understanding costs and cost control is very important in any business, large or small. Even though this might have been a "no-brainer" to most of you, it's important that you understand that **everything** has a monetary cost, even if it is hard to quantify. The extra touches of gold paint or ribbon on the shell, the time you spend on the Internet or at the library doing research, means cash is flowing out. If you donate a product or service what is your return? If not financial, will it be in publicity for you or your product? If none of the above applies, I'm sure it will look good as you enter the "Pearly Gates".

Create a <u>Projected Year One Balance Sheet</u>. This is designed to show what your company owns and owes. If you have an existing business and can do actual balance sheets, be sure the one you submit with your loan application is current (less than three months old). All Balance Sheets should have a section for your Assets, a section for your Liabilities, and a section that shows your Equity or the Capital you have invested in your company.

SAMPLE BALANCE SHEET

BALANCE SHEET FOR A START-UP COMPANY

Date

ASSETS

Cash	$20,000
Prepaid Insurance	1,000
Inventory	50,000
Equipment (less accumulated depreciation)	500
Deposits on furniture and utilities	<u>1,500</u>
Total assets	$73,000

LIABILITIES

Long term notes payable	$23,000

CAPITAL

Owners investment	<u>$50,000</u>
Total liability and owner's equity	$73,000

There are lots of models for more complicated business plans as near as your library, computer or neighborhood bookstore. Our Resource Section will list websites and books you can check out for a model that may meet your needs better than this one. However, you may want to "practice" with this simple outline. If you find this daunting, don't throw your money away at Barnes and Noble for a book on Business Plans you'll only use for a paperweight. Quite frankly, most lenders and ALL microlenders will be thrilled if you show up at their door with the information described in this outline neatly typed, packaged and ready for review. Don't make your life harder than it needs to be.

Carole Zavala Laidlaw

Judith Luther Wilder

Lindsay Shields

Mary Sullivan

Janet Trondle

Business Tip: Buy one good dress. Share the cost with four friends. Wear it for twenty years.

MARKETING

Marketing is one of those jobs many amateurs tackle with great confidence. Certain they can market their products better and cheaper than any high-priced marketing consultant or firm, they waste a lot of time, money and good will on marketing strategies no marketing professional would ever endorse. The same people who sensibly insist that their dentists and bankers have training and experience boldly plunge in where angels and experienced business people fear to tread. At the very least, I urge new business owners to bounce ideas about marketing their products off people who actually have sold something at some point in their lives. I also urge them to write a Marketing Plan if only because the process of creating a plan will make them think seriously about whether or not they are qualified to implement it.

An excellent and **free** Marketing Guide from Southern California Edison's Economic & Business Development Division defines Marketing as everything you do *before* and *after* a sale. I believe good marketing is essentially an extension of good manners (say Thank You when someone gives you money or supports your business) and good sense (say Thank You when someone gives you money or supports your business).

It is, in fact, everything you do to make your first sale as well as everything you do to ensure repeat business. Marketing also relates to what you do for your entire business rather than what you do to promote one product or service. Never kid yourself into thinking you can sell great lasagna if the salad, soup, dessert and coffee coming from your kitchen make your customers long for airline food.

In order to really get a handle on marketing your business, you should have a written plan. Your plan doesn't have to equal the Marketing Plan Microsoft will use to launch Windows 2010. However, like Bill-What Monopoly-Gates, you need to understand your products and services, you need to know who your customers and competitors are, you should have sales and revenue targets, and you should have some strategy and plan written down which addresses those sales and revenue targets.

The following pages will provide a short Marketing Plan outline. It is not meant to imply that you cannot or should not develop a plan that is more comprehensive. Rather, you should use the following outline as a point of departure. It is an illustration of the information you should assemble at minimum, before you wander into your neighborhood bank to ask some jaded loan officer to invest in your expertise and business.

This chapter will also include tips from Marketing professionals who have "been there, done that," specialists in marketing without much money who have helped sell everything from the odd to the obscene. Take their advice only if you are really serious about selling reconditioned computers to Third World secretarial schools or more tickets to your exhibition of rusty eyeglasses and antique Singer sewing machine bobbins.

Road Map For Selling Your Product, Service Or Creation

Think of your Marketing Plan as a road map that shows the paths to take as you prepare to sell your product or service. If you are an artist, explore the strategies you will use to persuade a gallery owner to represent you or the ways in which you will approach a theater manager who might present your dance company. It is all part of marketing and like it or not, you should be involved in the where, how and why your work and business are promoted.

Remember, Marketing Plans and Business Plans are living documents that should reflect the changes in your business environment. A good Marketing Plan will be updated at least annually and will adapt to changing trends, financial circumstances and your own changing lifestyle. Ten years ago Marketing Plans were written with the understanding they'd be set in concrete for five years. They were used to be based on an information stream that was very slow. Today information is instantly available so your Marketing Plan should be fluid. There is no excuse not to regularly review your plan with your partners, key employees and/or collaborators.

Step I

Define your business in terms people outside your business will understand. If you are a self-employed artist, try to think of your work in terms of your business and your goals in terms of the income you want to generate. Your creative goals and objectives are important but for the purpose of this exercise, concentrate on *the business of art*.

It is difficult to be too concise when describing your business. Students at the American Woman's Economic Development Corporation, an entrepreneurial training program founded in 1976 in New York by Beatrice Fitzpatrick, were always urged to describe their businesses in the amount of time it took an elevator to go from the first floor to the tenth floor. The theory was that you might meet a buyer/donor/angel on the run and if you couldn't describe your business in a very short period of time, you'd lose an opportunity to sell a product/attract an investor/secure a loan or a grant.

Define your business in ten words. If that's too painful, try twenty-five. Do not indulge yourself in breathless prose, poetry or long paragraphs.

An example used in the Southern California Edison Marketing Guide is an old tongue twister: She *sells seashells by the seashore*. If you can't resist rhetoric, you may want to say *She sells the best and most beautiful seashells by the seashore*.

Lee Bright, the author of The Bright Marketing Workbook and the owner of Bright Marketing International, defines her business in thirty-two very well chosen words: *Bright Marketing helps small to medium-size businesses increase their sales through targeted marketing efforts. We help your business grow at a rate to achieve your goals while staying within your budget.* Obviously the key phrases here are "increase sales" and "staying within your budget." There is not a client alive that will knowingly hire you to go over budget or to help it maintain the status quo.

Now you try it. Go ahead. Write a definition of your business. And because I'm an old softy, I'm going to grant you three lines and thirty-five words for this part of the exercise.

_____

_____

_____

Step II

Define Your Goals And Objectives. This is a tricky part of the Marketing drill. In order to do this, you have to set financial goals for Years One – Three (some banks may require five-year projections but start with a three-year overview). If you want to show an annual profit of $100,000 in three years, what do you realistically think you will see in profit in Year One? In order to achieve this, what do your annual sales need to be, how many employees do you need to achieve your $100,000 objective, and how many customers do you need to have? Try filling in the blanks in the following chart:

OBJECTIVES	1 YEAR	2 YEARS	3 YEARS
Market Share			
Customer Base			
Annual Sales			
Number of Employees			
Annual Profit			
Other			

Step III

Consider non-financial goals and objectives. Do you want to be known as the Public Relations agency for four of the five top women's organizations in the country? Do you want to have a national reputation for personal service? Do you want to have exhibitions in two major museums in the United States? Clarify your non-monetary goals and objectives as well and write them down.

My company will _____

_____

_____

Within three years my company will

_____

_____

Step IV

Clarify how your product, service or work is of benefit to your customers. For example, the desk chairs you sell may reduce fatigue, help eliminate backache, and last longer than other chairs sold at the same price. If your chairs are also a thing of beauty, state that but be careful not to confuse the benefits to the customer with a description of your product. If you are presenting the first performance of the post-war Cambodian Court Dancers in a venue outside Phnom Penh, you present a real benefit and opportunity for audiences to see an art form many feared had been extinguished in the wartime Killing Fields of Southeast Asia. If you list the names of the dancers and describe their costumes, you are only describing a feature of the work you're presenting. Try to be very clear when describing the benefits your product, service or work will bring to your customers and audiences.

My customers/clients/audiences benefit from my product/service/ work by

1._____

_____and

2._____

_____

Step V

Recognize that competition can be a major asset to your business. It is true that it is smarter to open a shoe store in an area with three other shoe stores than in an area with no shoe stores and a half-dozen used car lots. If there are four shoe stores located on one block, chances are very great that customers in search of shoes will be drawn to that block. It is also likely that at least two of the storeowners will have done their market research and made a conscious decision to open their shops on the same block. Which is not to say you should not do your own research. Conditions change and what was true in 1990 may not be true in 2001. You will also want to know if there is a particular niche market the existing shoe stores have overlooked.

It is critically important that bankers, investors, and/or donors are confident you understand your competition and the marketplace in which you propose to work. They will want to know you are knowledgeable about your competitor's product quality and price, the depth of their inventory, the kind of service they offer, and the ways in which they promote and advertise their product. If you can personally test the competition's products and service, you should. As a potential shoe store owner, walking a mile or two in another person's shoes makes good sense. If you're a choreographer and dance company director, you need to know who is presenting their work both before and after you hope to schedule your own work in a specific community. Find out how much other companies are charging for tickets, if they are promoting their performances through local dance schools and universities, and if they have special appeal to particular constituencies. Choreographer Liz Lerman, for example, often works with community residents and senior citizen populations.

If your dance company is creating a new work using untrained elderly dancers from the community, you probably won't want to immediately follow on Liz's talented heels into the same theater. Unless, of course, she's established a huge following of retired citizens eager to see their peers, under the direction of any choreographer, trip the light fantastic. Just be sure you make an *informed* decision.

Take the time to jot down the names of businesses or companies that offer products similar to yours in the area where you hope to work. List everything you know about their products, including information about price, reputation, service, quality and any unique features that work to their advantage. Also list their weaknesses and then compare your own products against those of your competition.

	YOUR COMPANY	COMPETITOR 1	COMPETITOR 2
Description of product			
Quality			
Price			
Service			
Reputation			
Unique Feature			
Promotional Strategies			

Step VI

Identify Your Market. This is as important as creating a good product. If there are no buyers for your product, it won't matter too much if your vegetable slicer slices faster, cleaner, and safer. Audiences have been developed in areas where everyone said it couldn't be done (the Shakespeare Festival in Ashland, Oregon, and the Opera House in Death Valley come to mind) but ideally, you will open your theater in an area which is inhabited by people who already enjoy live theater.

Breaking Through The Clutter

Identify and describe your customer. Who are the people who do not have to be persuaded, bribed or coerced into buying your paintings (on velvet) of Elvis in his early years? Who has been waiting impatiently for someone to create a new and better cookbook featuring rhubarb and tofu recipes? Determine early on if your niche market is too narrow. Perhaps rhubarb and tofu enthusiasts, albeit dedicated and loyal, are too few to make the million dollars you hoped to salt away by Labor Day. Or perhaps the market you've identified is too large and needs a little reeling in. If you've identified all of China as a potential market segment and you have $10,000 allocated for next year's direct mail campaign, promotional brochures, advertising and internet promotions, you may want to narrow your focus.

Concentrate your first efforts on customers who cost the least to reach and maintain. Spend one-third of your marketing dollars on testing new markets, and then use a portion of your resources to figure out what works and what doesn't.

In the early stages of your business, exploit all the free resources you have at your disposal. For example, much of your research can be covered through information you can obtain through Small Business Development Centers and the United States Small Business Administration.

Other **free** and low-cost ways to learn about your customers include trade association reports, your competitors' annual reports, competitors' ads and literature, and an Internet usernet newsgroup or list serve which addresses your particular market.

Lee Bright suggests going right to the source for good information about what your customers like. Creating a questionnaire for your existing customers, says Lee, will not only tell you who your ideal customer is but what they like or don't like about your product, service, or performance.

In her 1996 *Bright Marketing Workbook* she developed two versions (one for individuals and one for businesses) of a questionnaire which she asked her customers to complete. Once the questionnaires were collected, she shared them with her employees so they would also begin to get a sense of Bright International Marketing's ideal customer. By sorting the questionnaires according to gender, type of business, dollars spent, it became immediately clear which customers required the least amount of time and produced the maximum amount of business. Like most businesses, Bright International Marketing generates 80% of its business from the top 20% of its customers.

Lee's two sample questionnaires and her assessment notes may be of assistance to you as you begin to research who your customers are and why they support your business:

THE BRIGHT MARKETING WORKBOOK

Dear Valued Customer:

In order for us to provide the best possible service to you, we need your assistance. Please complete the following questionnaire and leave it with the receptionist before you leave today. To show our appreciation for taking this time, we'll be happy to provide you with a discount of $3.00 off your purchase of any retail product upon completion of the questionnaire.

Your help will provide necessary information for us to continue providing you with the quality service and products you have come to expect from us. We appreciate you!

Name_____Address_____

City, State,

Zip_____

Phone (please indicate Res or Bus)_____

How often do you dine in restaurants?

    Once a month   Twice a month   Once a week   More often than once a week

Please list your favorite restaurant(s) in the area: _____

_____

How often do you go to local movie theaters?

    2-3 times a year   Once a month   2 times a month   Once a week

What newspaper do you read regularly?   None   LA Times

    Wall Street Journal   LA Business Journal   Grunion Gazette

Please list your favorite radio station: _____

_____

Do you watch cable television in our area?   Yes   No

If Yes, how often?   Periodically   Twice a week   Every day

Please list any particular shows you watch frequently: _____

_____

What do you like most about our store?_____

_____

What improvements can we make?_____

_____

What additional products or services would you like to see offered? _____

If your perfect customer is a business, your questionnaire might look something like this:

Name_____ Title_____

Company_____

City, State,

Zip_____

Phone (please indicate Res or Bus)_____

What publications do you subscribe to?   None   LA Times

   Wall Street Journal   Business Week   Inc.   Other

Please list your favorite radio station: _____

Do you watch cable television in our area?   Yes   No

If Yes, how often?   Periodically   Twice a week   Every day

 Please list any particular shows you watch frequently: _____

_____

Do you attend industry trade shows?   Yes   No

 If Yes, which ones? _____

What do you like most about our product/service?_____

_____

How would you rate our service?   Excellent   Good   Needs work

What improvements can we make?_____

_____

What additional products or services would you like to see offered? _____

_____

After your customers have completed and returned these questionnaires, distribute them to your employees (or do this part of the exercise yourself), and make notes on the bottom or back of the questionnaire to include estimates of:

If your customers are individuals

Age_____Income Level_____Gender_____

Works outside the home   Yes   No

Types of products purchased/services used_____
_____
_____

How often frequents the store/business?_____

Estimated purchases in last six months $_____

If your customers are businesses

Years in business_____Annual Revenue_____

Types of products purchased/services used_____
_____

How often frequents the store/business? _____

Estimated purchases in last six months $_____

Once the questionnaires are finished, sort them into categories by gender, type of business, or other pertinent qualifier, and dollars spent. You will see very quickly who your PERFECT customers are. If you have decided NOT to use the questionnaire, you can use the following as a guide to preparing your perfect customer list. Add other pertinent information, depending on the nature of your business and client base.

$$ Spent/Billed in past six months_____

Products/services purchased_____

_____

Age_____ or Years in Business_____

Income Level_____ or Annual Sales_____

Marital Status_____or Title _____

Geographic Location _____

Business/Profession _____

As Lee suggests, before all else fails, ASK your customers why they hire you, why they like your product or production and if they have thoughts about how you can improve your service to them. Ask them for information on how best to reach them, if the price is right, how you can improve access and delivery and if they are as likely or more likely to support your competition. Remember to always ask your most important questions first. I don't know about your client base but my friend's clients and customers have a very short attention span. They may or may not finish filling out a long questionnaire. If there's any doubt whether or not they'll make it to page three, front load your questionnaire with the questions you most want to have answered.
You should also urge them to honestly and critically evaluate your strengths and weaknesses and if you can, reward them for their time and effort on your behalf. As I said in the chapter *Getting Started*, "give regular customers a free squirrel's tail now and then. It makes them feel good and the squirrel is already dead."

Step VII

Remember Pricing Should Be Both Competitive And Profitable. There are many ways to price your product or service but you must always keep the concept of supply and demand in mind. Do you have the only shoe store in town? Are there three shoe stores on your block? It's important to remember to cover your costs but you must also price your shoes to make a profit. Don't set your price too low just to make a sale.

If the competition offers a lower price than you do, think about other services you can offer. Can you provide a delivery service so that the customer doesn't have to carry packages around while shopping for groceries? Can you give a discount if two or more pairs of shoes are purchased? What can you do to justify a slightly higher price? Surveys repeatedly indicate that service and quality are more important to a consumer than price but they have to be convinced the service and quality really are superior.

When my partners and I founded Women Incorporated we chose to identify our company as the AARP for women entrepreneurs. AARP, the American Association for Retired Persons, is arguably the most powerful lobby in Washington and the largest association in the country. Because its numbers are so large and because they have a number of profit centers, they can afford to charge very low membership fees. Women Incorporated did not want money to be a barrier to membership and following AARP's lead, publicly positioning itself as an organization any woman business owner could afford to join. For $29 a year, any member, man or woman, could receive a slew of benefits and discounts, a quarterly magazine, a bi-monthly newsletter, access to a National Financial Network, group rate health insurance, and access to a number of educational conferences, seminars and publications.

An annual membership fee of $29 would have worked out fine if we had started with 100,000 members. However, with only 10,000 members at the end of the first year, we were losing about $125 per member. This meant that most of the principals in the company spent most of their time fundraising to fill the gap between what each member paid and what each member cost. Not a good use of our time but a wonderful example of what can happen when you don't take the time to write a Marketing Plan. If we had done our Pricing and Sales Projection exercises, we'd have either charged a much higher membership fee or gone into the aluminum siding business.

Step VIII

Design Your Marketing Strategies and Tactics. This information is at the heart of every Marketing Plan. The specific strategies you design and the tactics you use to implement your strategies will depend on your budget, your previous experience and what is appropriate for your customers. Obviously you wouldn't use Marilyn Manson to recruit for Pat Robertson's college programs. However, you may want to use a Marilyn Manson endorsement if you're firing up a campaign to sell grunge clothing to dysfunctional teens. Again, the information you gather from your questionnaires will tell you a lot about how best to reach your ideal customer. If your surveys tell you most of your customers are college students who regularly read the college newspaper, advertising in college newspapers makes perfect sense.

Strategies common to most businesses include efforts to expand their customer base, increase sales, decrease costs, and to sell more products, tickets and services to the customers they have. In your Marketing Plan, state the strategies that will help achieve your goals and then describe the tactics you will use to implement your strategies.

For example, if your strategy is to sell more tickets to a performance of The Children Of Bali, your Marketing Plan should include the following information:

NAME OF THE PERFORMANCE	Children of Bali Dance Company
MARKET NICHE	Dance students, teachers, Indonesian people living in Los Angeles, World Music and World Dance aficionados, audience members who have supported previous World Dance Festivals.
STRATEGY	Sell tickets to previous customers plus expand audiences by 25%.
TACTICS	Direct mail to lists of previous World Dance and World Music subscribers, dance and music faculty members, and dance students; Advertisements in university and Indonesian newspapers; Bulletin Board postings in Dance and Music departments; Internet postings to travel agencies specializing in Bali or Java; Distribution of brochures to Indonesian Consulate, university dance departments, travel agencies specializing in travel to Bali and Java; Indonesian restaurants.

Your written plan should also include the following information about Implementation:

Activity	Distribution of brochures
Date activity (such as mailing) will be carried out	May 1
Name of person responsible for activity	Nyoman Suparwita
Budget for implementing activity	$600 for printing; $400 for labor; $50 for gas for volunteers

Step IX

Make Realistic Sales Projections. These projections are a key part of your Marketing Plan and provide an opportunity to persuade lenders and investors that you know everything there is to know about your customers and your product.

The following questions should all be addressed in this section of your plan:

- Is your business wholesale or retail?
- Can you describe your sales approach realistically?
- Will you have a sales staff and how will they be compensated?
- Will you offer discounts and incentives for your customers and/or sales people?
- How will you estimate the cost of your work and/or producing your product?
- Will you require advance payments and retainers?
- Do you have sample sales contracts?
- Who in your company is responsible for sales activity?
- What are your sales objectives? How many sales do you need to make weekly in order for your business to show a profit?

Make sure your sales projections are conservative. Do not do your lender or yourself a disservice by being overly optimistic. If you're selling tickets to a performance, make your projections based on filling 50% of the seats. If you're selling oranges by the bushel, be realistic about spoilage, theft, and loss.

Filling out the following chart will be helpful to you in developing your marketing budget. It will also be useful as an evaluation tool as you compare projections to actuals at the end of your season or year:

SALES PROJECTIONS FOR _____ *(fill in product or service)*

| | DATA | | | %CHANGE | |
	Last Year	This Year	Next Year	From Last Year to This Year	From This Year to Next Year
#present customers					
Number of sales					
Units/Customer					
Total units					
Price per unit					
Sales revenues from present customers					
# new customers					
Number of sales					
Units/Customer					
Total units					
Price per unit					
Sales revenues from new customers					
Sales revenues from all customers					
MARKET SHARE (%)					

Step X

Describe Your Financial and Staff Resources. A good Marketing Plan is a wonderful tool but you have to let your lender or donor know how much it will cost to implement it, and which of your many competent staff members will be responsible for turning your words into reality. Each program or activity you've described will need a dollar figure attached to it. One way of looking at what is reasonable to spend on your marketing efforts may be based on your number of customers and what they spend. Review your sales projections in the previous chart and create a Marketing Budget that strikes a conservative balance with your Sales Projections.

The following chart will be helpful to you as you complete this exercise:

MARKETING BUDGET			
ITEM	*YEAR 1*	*YEAR 2*	*YEAR 3*
Salaries, Marketing			
Salaries, Sales			
Direct Mail			
Advertising			
Public Relations			
Trade Shows			
Outside Consultants			
Indirect Costs			
Other			
Total Costs for Marketing Budget			

The next step in your Marketing Plan will involve **Promotion** and for the purpose of this book, includes Public Relations, Press Relations and Advertising activities, all covered at length in the following Chapter.

Final Words To The Wise

Everyone moves at hyper-speed in most areas of America today and entrepreneurs are among the worst offenders. We spend so much time developing our product or service, finding and selling to customers and then racing at breakneck speed to find and sell to new ones that niceties like Thank You notes get left in the dust. If gratitude is expressed, it tends to be expressed in a form letter. I believe it is an Absolute Truth that people who write personal Thank You notes today stand out head and shoulders above the rest of us. There is no marketing effort that comes close to producing so big a bang for the buck.

A few years ago Women Incorporated produced a conference that engaged over a hundred highly qualified and compelling volunteer speakers. Most of them came to the conference at their own expense, some spent the night at local hotels and several incurred the cost of airfare in order to support our cause. The least we could do, we felt, was write personal Thank You notes to all the speakers expressing our appreciation for sharing their expertise and wisdom with thousands of entrepreneurial hopefuls.

My partner and I painstakingly drafted dozens of versions of letters so that a speaker who flew from Jamaica would not receive the same letter as the Mayor of Long Beach or the former Governor of Texas. Unfortunately, we did not draft one hundred different Thank You letters. When they finally went out, many of the letters had secretarial notations indicating that ten or eleven other speakers were receiving the very same letter. Not only did the notes not carry with them the spirit of sincere appreciation we truly felt but they also represented a great waste of time and opportunity.

I suppose the moral to this story is that the road to Hell is paved with good intentions and that we should never take on a job or a project if we're going to do it in a half-assed way. Our job clearly was not done when we finished drafting the letters. We should have spent as much time and effort reviewing each letter as we'd spent in drafting the invitations to speak and we should never have signed twenty and thirty letters while we were simultaneously conducting unrelated business on the phone.

At the other end of the spectrum, I must tell you that I have a thin file of wonderful letters, several handwritten, from very busy people who took the time to thank me for some minor good deed. And while I long ago forgot the good deeds that inspired the notes, I treasure the beautiful hand-written message from Caroline Ahmanson, the Grand Dame and Cultural Conscience of Los Angeles; the kind words from East Coast Public Relations Maven Terri Williams, and a wonderful note from artist Meredith Monk. I also treasure the sweet notes I have received from students and interns over the years, notes that, without exception, always moved me to some sort of positive action on their behalf. My own response to these written expressions of appreciation convinces me that almost anyone can distinguish himself from the hurrying hordes merely by taking the time to write a few words which say "Thank You for supporting my work, for buying my product, for purchasing my service."

Good manners and good sense may not be everything but if you don't have either, you won't have much of a Marketing Plan nor much of a business.

Marketing Tips That Won't Cost A Fortune To Implement

1. Become an expert. Television, radio, the Internet, and newspapers are always looking for experts to quote. Become an accessible expert who is available for interviews.

2. Join advertising forces with others. Persuade your manufacturer or supplier to share advertising costs with you or ask a group of other merchants or arts organizations to share the cost of producing and financing ads.

3. Get a marketing intern to take you on as a client. It will give you free marketing assistance and will give the intern some professional experience.

4. Carry business cards with you all day, every day. Give prospective clients two cards, one to keep and one to pass along.

5. Develop a site on the World Wide Web. It's inexpensive and has the potential to reach a lot of people, and everybody and their pet pigs, including IBM, wants to help you do it.

6. Submit "tip" articles to newspaper and client newsletters.

7. Send hand-written Thank You cards, birthday cards, and seasonal greeting cards.

8. Write an ad in another language to reach a non-English speaking market. Place the ad in a publication that market reads. (This is an effective marketing tool but it has to be done right. Hilarious mistakes have been made by very large companies hoping to reach foreign markets. A famous ad became a famous gaffe when it was translated into Chinese as "Nothing sucks like Electrolux.")

9. Network, network, network. Join the Chamber of Commerce, a trade association or a breakfast club with professionals not in your field who can make business referrals for you. Remain open to going new places and meeting new people. Business opportunities pop up in the most surprising places.

10. Create and pass out Rolodex cards or telephone stickers preprinted with your business contact information.

11. Use colored or oversized envelopes for your direct mail.

12. Be the nicest shoe storeowner on the block. Answer all calls as soon as possible. Be courteous and train your employees and associates to treat everyone with respect. Remember that service is more important to customers than price and that attitude is damn near everything!

Margo Upham of Upham & Associates with another satisfied customer

PROMOTION

Dr. Marsha Firestone, president of the Women Presidents' Organization, a national non-profit association of women CEOs, co-authored a book for Women Incorporated entitled *The Busy Woman's Guide To Successful Self-Employment"*. Together with Bernard Fortunoff, the president and chief operating officer for the prestigious Masters Institute in California's Silicon Valley, Dr. Firestone developed a comprehensive guide for women planning to embark as self-employed entrepreneurs. The guide's chapters on Promotion and developing Business Plans provide the clearest, most concise advice on these topics I've read in any business book over the past ten years. Since it is highly unlikely I can improve on their efforts, the following chapter will, with the authors' approval, borrow shamelessly from *The Busy Woman's Guide To Successful Self-Employment.*

The chapter also includes information and tips from the excellent public relations professionals I met during the time I was employed as the Director of the American Woman's Economic Development Corporation in California and from Margo Upham, president of Upham & Associates, a public relations firm in Los Angeles.

The advice given in the following pages is also colored by my own minor successes and colossal failures as an occasional public relations director over the past two decades.

Promotion is everything you do to contact and persuade your customers (or clients or audience members) to become your customers, to buy what you are selling and to return for repeat business.

Basic promotional methods include public relations, press relations, sales promotions and personal sales. An entire promotional campaign can be based on what your company represents. Federal Express is an excellent example of a company that developed its promotional strategy around one theme: fast service.

Firestone and Fortunoff suggest that all good promotion plans should begin by answering the following five questions:

1. To whom do you want to communicate?
2. What information do you want to communicate?
3. What are the most effective methods of reaching the right audience with the right message?
4. What media should be used?
5. How much money can be allocated for effective promotion?

Promotion starts with a good name. A name that advertises your business, is easy to pronounce, isn't already taken and doesn't cause an international crisis when non-English speaking people see it is a good place to start.

There are classic examples of bad names for good products. A few years ago I heard about a family from Europe who opened a diner in North Hollywood. Proud of their Dalmatian homeland in Eastern Europe, they had a huge sign made to hang across the entrance of their small restaurant. Much to the dismay of their friends and prospective customers,"HOME OF THE DALMATIAN BURGER"was emblazoned across the sign, their menus and their promotional flyers. This unfortunately occurred during the re-release of Disney's "101 Dalmatians". Horrified children and parents avoided the new diner by the thousands.

The Chevy Nova is an example of a name that did not play well in all communities. Spanish-speaking populations in both Mexico and the United States may have admired Chevy's efforts to bring truth to advertising but since the name indicated the car wouldn't go, it wasn't one of Chevrolet's best sellers in Spanish-speaking communities.

Creating a consistent look for your business is as important as a good name. A strong graphic image of your name and logo should be used on your business cards, your signs, your letterhead, your brochures, and in your advertising. If you are short of cash and long on talent and can design your own logo, do it. If you have graphics software that enables you to produce an attractive design, make that work for you. Design students at local colleges may also help you design business materials in exchange for samples of finished products to add to their portfolios. However you manage it, get an image that not only represents your business but will wear well over time.

Once you have your business materials in place, you can move on to promotional activities such as public and press relations. It is always easier, of course, to hand these tasks off to experienced professionals but if you're just starting out and your budget is very tight, you may have to learn how to do everything yourself. As in most things in life, the best advice I can give you is to "keep it simple".

Almost everyone in the art world resents the type of artist who indulges in "hype" but no one I know in the media or in an arts management position resents artists who provide them with straightforward, timely information. Communicating with journalists, critics, and radio/television staff people who run free public service announcements is just another chore artists have to take on if they want people outside their families to know about what they're doing.

From 1983 to 1986, my company coordinated a performance art series in Los Angeles called EXPLORATIONS. Although the responsibility for promoting and publicizing the series rested with my office, the responsibility for supplying us with publicity materials rested with the artists. Of the twenty-eight artists and groups we handled during the three-year series, no one made our work quite as easy as performance artist and future co-founder of Highways (a performance space in Santa Monica, California), Tim Miller. If we asked for pictures, we'd get three black and white photographs shot from different angles and a half-dozen color transparencies. If we asked for copies of reviews, we'd get them in the next mail delivery, and if we asked for videotape for television, Federal Express would deliver it the next day. Other artists in the series, such as Meredith Monk, Eric Bogosian, and Paul Dresher, were also conscientious about providing us the tools we needed to do a good job for them. Tim, however, was particularly impressive because he operated as a one-man publicist/business agent/technical director/artist. Which is exactly what most young artists or entrepreneurs starting out must be prepared to do.

As a one-woman or one-man Promotions Strategist, you will have to handle Public Relations, Press Relations, and Advertising until the lucky day when you can afford to hire professional assistance. The following tips are meant for beginners and have been gathered from a number of impressive sources, including Firestone and Fortunoff :

Public Relations is all about the image you present to customers, suppliers, colleagues, audiences and the general public. As in most areas of business, common sense should dictate the approach you take when you design a Public Relations strategy for your company. For example:

- Remember that your reputation is your primary currency. Make certain that you never compromise your good name.
- Keep your promises. If you promise a customer a discount or an early delivery, be absolutely certain you can follow through on your promise.
- Give your brochure or sales materials to people who depend on you for work and support. Your lawyer, accountant, printer, banker, and advertising consultant should all have several copies of your company brochure and business card.
- Extend your hours of operation. Museums often appear to structure their hours of operation for the convenience of the museum staff. Ensure a competitive edge by letting the public know your business is open when your competitors are not. If most of your customers are available in the evenings and on weekends, they need to know your business can serve them during these times.
- Ask former clients why they left you and don't argue with them when they answer your questions. Whether their reasons are valid or not, their perceptions are relevant and they should be thanked for giving you valuable information.
- Establish a marketing/public relations advisory and referral team composed of colleagues or business associates. Treat them to lunch every other month.
- Include reviews or testimonials from satisfied customers in all your promotional literature.
- Maintain a "tickler file" for ideas you may not use today but can use when you have more time, more money, and more staff.
- Listen when people are talking to you. Don't let your eyes wander to the super star or major donor talking to your competitor across the room.
- Send congratulatory notes to customers, vendors, even competitors when they have accomplished something or reached some personal or business milestone.
- Volunteer. Every good job I've ever had came my way through contacts I had made or experience I gained as a volunteer. These jobs include the directorship of a $5 million festival, a position as the Superintendent of Cultural Affairs for a large city, and teaching positions at two universities. I've also secured many more contracts and clients through my volunteer activities than through more traditional ways of marketing my company. This is, of course, not the purpose of volunteering but giving time for a cause in which you believe can certainly provide a lot of wonderful and surprising side benefits.

If you are a self-employed artist, personal letters of invitation to critics, public service announcements, flyers, posters, post cards and targeted mailing lists will all play a part in developing support for your art. Just as entrepreneurs have to create a market for their products and services, you will have to create a demand for your work.

If you're lucky, you will have a network of family members, friends, and colleagues who will help you as you get to know curators, collectors and gallery owners. At the start of your career, you may have a support system of one and it may fall on *you* to do everything Tim Miller, Eric Bogosian, Eleanor Academia-Magda and most other artists have had to do at the beginning of their careers.

It is time-consuming work and it takes time and talent to do it well. It is also necessary work. No one will come to your studio and drop offers and money in your lap. On the day you decide to become a professional artist, you should also begin the process of self-promotion.

You can begin by attending art events and openings where you'll meet other artists, arts patrons and the arts press. By exchanging business cards over cheap white wine, you can begin building a mailing list. Eventually you will develop a list of people with a genuine interest in the arts and when you add the new names to your list of relatives, your dentist, the neighbors and your parent's best friends, you will discover you have a respectable support system.

You should also begin assembling materials for a promotional package or press kit. Reviews, your resume, slides, photographs, press releases, and any articles written about you or your work should all go into your file. When you have enough materials to make a favorable impression, you can create a package to send to curators, gallery owners and presenters. Whether you are seeking an exhibition, a grant, or sales, you will need to have a package that represents you and your work. There are too many good, accessible artists around competing for the attentions and limited resources of curators and presenters. Don't make it hard for them to find you or to figure out what you do. They may not make the effort when a Bill Viola or a Pattsi Valdez is just a phone call away.

While promotion *is* necessary, you're going to be yesterday's news if your work is not solid, honest and original. So keep it all in perspective. You do need to learn to present yourself professionally but you must always stay in touch with the reason for the press release and promotional kits. When you spend more time working as a publicist than as an artist and when your press packets outshine your art, you had better do some soul-searching and determine if you've confused the business of art with the art of business.

If you own a very small company, your Press Relations activities may be limited to getting press releases out to print and broadcast media. Almost every bookstore or library will have dozens of books with chapters on the elements of a good press release. The website for the Public Relations Society of America will also provide you with a wealth of information about press relations. If you want to save yourself a trip to the nearest Barnes & Noble, check out their site at www.prsa.org.

Since journalists receive hundreds of press releases daily, it will behoove you to keep your press release brief, factual and free of jargon. Generally, the rules to follow are simple:

- Write **PRESS RELEASE** at the top-center of the page under the letterhead. **CONTACT NAME** and **PHONE NUMBER** should be at the top-left corner of the
- page. **FOR IMMEDIATE RELEASE** should be at the top-right corner of your release unless the release is meant for a later date.
- Summarize all-important information in the beginning of the release. The reader should be able to figure out what is going on in the first paragraph.
- Try to limit your release to one page and under no circumstances make it longer than two pages. The end of the war in Kosovo may warrant a three-page release but the appearance of a performing artist or the introduction of a new software package does not.
- It is acceptable to include a fact sheet and/or photo with your one-page release. Include only facts and no quotes or testimonials. All photos should be captioned Who, What, Where, When and Why. Captions can be attached to the photo on a separate piece of paper.
- If you must write a two-page release, end page one with a complete sentence. Type "-more-" in the bottom-center of the first page so the reader will know he is to read on. At the top of the second page, on either the left or right of the page, write the name of your company, the date, page number and topic of the release.
- Write "end" or "####" at the end of your release so the reader will know there is no additional text to follow.
- Type on only one side of the paper and always double space the text.
- Finally, make certain the story you are pitching is newsworthy. Don't waste your time on a "puff piece" unless you're specifically targeting a publication that specializes in running vanity pieces.

Once you've submitted your release to a newspaper or radio/television station, it's appropriate to follow-up and make sure it was received. Be organized when you call and always begin the conversation by asking if the reporter is on a deadline. If the answer is Yes, ask for a good time to call back. If the answer is No, be ready to make your pitch in no longer than two minutes.

In their chapter on **Advertising**, Firestone and Fortunoff suggest that "doing business without Advertising is like winking at a girl in the dark. You know what you're doing but no one else does."

Adrienne Hall, co-owner of the first woman-owned advertising company in the country, says that whereas Advertising once comprised 90% of all Marketing, Advertising today accounts for less than 30% of the average company's entire Marketing budget. She notes the increasing importance of the Internet, particularly to artists who can create their own brands. Licensing, sponsorships, and sports and entertainment marketing also play an important role in branding for corporations and even for small businesses.

"In a recent report presented by the American Advertising Federation," says Hall, "major corporate clients shocked their advertising agencies by ranking advertising sixth on a list of marketing strategies."

According to Margo Upham, "advertising is what you pay for and good public relations is what you pray for." Both require great expertise. While you can and actually may have to do the work yourself when you're first starting in business, you should always hire professional help as soon as you can afford it. Your company's image and its survival may rest on the way you handle Advertising and PR.

There may not be a company in the world that has winked in the dark more than Women Incorporated (WI). WI suffered serious setbacks because our Public Relations strategy was so fragmented and because we foolishly did not budget anything for advertising. In retrospect, a place where everyone has 20/20 vision, we should have known that budgeting for advertising was as important as budgeting for taxes or computer equipment. Although large corporations may still be spending one-third of their marketing dollars on advertising, a good rule of thumb for an advertising budget is 3% of gross sales for a retail business and 10% for a service business. I doubt that we ever spent one half of one percent of our annual budget for advertising.

If I could go back in time and create an advertising strategy for WI, this is what I would try and remember:

- One ad is just slightly more effective than the wink in the dark. The name of the game is repetition. Create an advertising campaign that includes a series of ads if you are serious about getting the customer's attention.
- You have to give something away. Always have specialty items such as coffee mugs, pens or mouse pads with your company logo on hand to give away at trade shows, conferences, or at special events. You should also have a good supply of samples and innovative items or "bumps" to mail to your prospect list. (A "bump" is something you can put in a mailing envelope to make it bulge and thus pique the recipient's curiosity.)
- It is important to participate in trade shows and conferences attended by your target market. Budget for eye-catching display materials or a booth as well as for exhibition fees and trained employees or company representatives to staff your display at as many fairs and trade shows as possible.
- Research data is the mother's milk of advertising. Know the age, average income, the cultural background, and the location of your target market. You should also know as much as possible about their lifestyle, their shopping habits and if they get their information from newspapers, magazines, television, the Internet, or radio.
- Evaluate your advertising efforts by tracking each ad you run. Always ask your customers where they heard about your company.

Tracking Costs

The worksheets developed by Dr. Firestone and Mr. Fortunoff for Women Incorporated's *Busy Woman's Guide To Successful Self-Employment* are excellent for tracking costs. They are also useful for assessing whether or not your marketing and promotional efforts are balanced. Chances are good that you won't be doing the business you want to do if you depend entirely on free listings and media coverage. If you are serious about doing business, you'd better get serious about promoting your business with all the tools at your disposal, including press relations, public relations and paid advertising.

ADVERTISING WORKSHEET
Cost of Newspaper and Magazine Advertising

Total Annual Budget: $_____
Estimate your advertising costs using these forms

Newspaper or Magazine	Sales Rep	Phone Number	Closing Dates	Line Rate	Ad Size	Cost Per Ad
1.						
2.						
3.						
4.						
5.						
6.						
7.						
8.						
9.						
10.						

Newspaper Or Magazine	Audience Demographics
1.	
2.	
3.	
4.	
5.	
6.	
7.	
8.	
9.	
10.	

$ 95

Marketing Budget for Business Image, Promotion, Advertising, and Public Relations
Cost Per Month

	Jan	Feb	Mar	Apr	May	Jun	Jul	Aug	Sep	Oct	Nov	Dec	Total
Business Image Logo Design Stationery Business Cards Announcements Signs Other													
Listings Yellow Pages Chamber Directory Business and Trade Directories													
Advertising Newspapers Magazines Flyers Radio Television Direct Mail Internet Trade Magazines Other													
Public Relations Releases Donations of Prizes Booths at Fairs Newsletters Open House Other													
Consultant Fees													

IF YOU WANT TO BE HAPPY AND SUCCESSFUL AND YOU DON'T WANT TO DIE ALONE, FOLLOW THESE THREE RULES!

Anyone who reaches the age of fifty has a pretty well formulated set of rules by which they live. This is particularly true of business people. It is virtually impossible to move through a bookstore these days without confronting a book of tips from a thirty-two year old entrepreneur who made three million dollars weaving place mats from old inner tubes.

SUCCESS, FORBES, ENTREPRENEUR, and WORKING WOMAN magazines all regularly feature articles by people of indisputable character and success who will share tricks guaranteed to get you and your twelve closest relatives a rich piece of the pie. They will all show you how to eat your cake and have it too. Occasionally, they'll even tell you how to grab and hold onto both the bird in the hand and the ten desperate sparrows caught in the bush.

The fact is, any reasonably intelligent person of a certain age and experience can give you good advice. They just can't make you take it. My advice is not significantly different from the advice you'd get from the thirty-two year old with a garage full of old inner tubes. Only the genesis is different. My advice comes from experiences I had in Cambodia between 1992 - 1999 as well as from watching a few thousand friends and colleagues over a period of twenty years succeed, fail and start over in business. The 32-year-old's advice comes from having incredible luck, a genius for marketing and a large supply of old rubber.

While I recognize following *my* three rules may not guarantee you fame, fortune and fulfillment, I can guarantee that you'll end up lonely and whining like a forlorn hooker at a Mormon convention in Salt Lake City if you don't follow them. My advice has also been endorsed by a well-known film producer with a personal fortune of two hundred million dollars, an artist who has exhibited at The Museum of Contemporary Art in Los Angeles and the Whitney in New York, and a wealthy 1999 Woman Entrepreneur of the World who started her company at home with an investment of $5000. For what it's worth, my grandmother and six-year-old grandson also think I make a lot of sense.

Rule Number 1: Learn to bury your dead and try to forgive. Everyone.

If I didn't know it before, one of the lessons I learned from my travels in Cambodia is that you can't move on if you're consumed with a hunger for revenge. If you carry a grudge around like a dog with a bone, you'll never be the entrepreneur, the artist, or the person you want to be. Grudges distract you from your work and drain you of creativity. Forget them.

There is not one positive thing you can say about people who "keep score" and are unforgiving. I don't mean to say that you should overlook the Holocaust or our deplorable history in Southeast Asia but I do think it is critical to bury your dead and move on. Forgive your father, your mother, the chippy who stole your boyfriend in the tenth grade, the business partner who stole your idea and your thunder, and the ex-husband (or ex-wife) who ran off with your best friend and left you with an $80,000 debt and three weeks of dirty laundry.

Cambodia As A Case Study

When I first began visiting Cambodia in 1992, I was, like most visitors during that period, almost paralyzed by the national sorrow that hung like a shroud over Phnom Penh. I was also completely confounded by the determination with which the survivors of both the Pol Pot atrocities and the Vietnamese occupation carried on. Even in those days, streets were crowded with merchants, motorbikes, and every means of transportation it was possible to devise. Restaurants and dance clubs were doing a booming business, and new hotels and shops were being created daily amidst two decades of rubble.

Still, there was and is today, ample evidence of the tragedy that wiped out almost a third of the country's population. Amputees by the hundreds, maybe thousands, were reduced to begging in the streets. A museum featuring haunting photographs of Pol Pot's victims was a major and grisly tourist attraction and monuments of human skulls could be found in every village we visited outside Phnom Penh.

Yet amidst all the horror and testimony of the dead and the living, one had the feeling Life was going to triumph. The University was packed with students eager to greet a new technological era as well as with art students committed to recapturing the music and dance of past centuries. Each night discos throughout the city were crowded with foreigners and Cambodians committed to absorbing the music and dance from this century. Every dance from the waltz to the lambada was demonstrated a dozen times a night by someone on those shiny new dance floors. Busy floating restaurants bobbed along the edges of the Mekong and shopkeepers haggled merrily with hopeful UN troops and NGO workers over $20 ruby and gold earrings.

It was therefore no real shock when it became clear that neither the government nor the people of Cambodia planned to hold war crime tribunals. Although everyone seemed to hold Pol Pot and his senior officers responsible for the deaths that had touched virtually every Cambodian household, few seemed to have time for a formal program of revenge.

This attitude had nothing to do with an absence of war criminals to try. Khmer Rouge defectors seemed to be everywhere in those days. Even Hun Sen, the current Prime Minister originally installed by the Vietnamese, had once been a member of a Khmer Rouge cadre. The trade school my friends built in one of the southern provinces of Cambodia enrolled, without incident, several former Khmer Rouge soldiers in their entrepreneurial training programs. In addition, artists thought to be puppets of the Vietnamese occupation worked in concert with artists who had struggled to keep their art alive in Thai refugee camps. In 1992 the country was a hodgepodge of heroes, artists, soldiers, farmers, criminals, survivors and overseas Cambodians returning to work on the country's first free elections. Except for the occasional politician, few seemed interested in either classifying or licking the country's truly horrendous wounds.

I don't suggest that everyday life in Cambodia was, by any sane standard, peaceful. Skirmishes between the Khmer Rouge hold outs and government troops continued in both the Northern and Southern provinces and the Royally Dysfunctional Family held its own skirmishes in the public arena. Whenever Khmer Rouge generals tried to enter Phnom Penh to explore opportunities for repatriation, they would have the shit beaten out of them and end up fleeing for their lives. Leaders of political parties regularly tossed hand grenades into their opponents' campaign headquarters and bickering went on between French Cambodians, American Cambodians, and Cambodians who had stayed behind during the worst of the tragedies.

That said, I did not see much evidence that the survivors' rage extended to rank and file Khmer Rouge. Even in 1992, the climate in Phnom Penh, a city that grew almost overnight from a ghost town to an urban center with one traffic light and a million people, was characterized by a powerful determination to bury the dead and get on with the business of living. No one I ever met said "I won't sell rice or eggs to that person because he was in the Khmer Rouge."

I don't pretend to understand the Cambodian psyche, but in that small and tortured Third World country, the shroud of sorrow was somehow interwoven with a surprisingly strong veil of hope.

Forgiving may be inadequate as a one-word description of the Cambodian people in the early '90's, but if acceptance, hope, and a tacit agreement to work side-by-side with your tormentors play any part in forgiveness, then the Cambodian people proved themselves to be forgiving. They were also contentious, volatile, frustrating and ultimately, wise enough to make a conscious decision to spend more time looking forward than back.

From that first of many visits to Cambodia, I left determined to never again cling to a grudge for either real or imagined insults and offenses to my sensibilities or my business. If my friends in Cambodia could move beyond the crimes of Pol Pot and the total abandonment of the rest of the world, I reasoned, I could overlook whatever Fate had in store for me as a businesswoman working in America. Even today, eight years after that first journey, I find myself embarrassed if I brood for more than five minutes about hurt feelings or someone reneging on a contract. In the big scheme of things and in the real world, **none of that really matters.**

This is, of course, a lesson that the most successful businessmen usually learn without stopping off in Southeast Asia. There's a line in the Broadway show "Annie" which has been paraphrased and used in a hundred speeches and is relevant to almost any time and situation: *"You don't have to be nice to people on the way up if you're not coming back down,"* says Daddy Warbucks. Most businessmen recognize that the ladder to the top is very slippery and hedge their bets by not carrying too much baggage as they climb.

Revenge Is Not A Business Strategy

It's not unusual in corporate America to see a top CEO of one company move to lead the troops of a former competitor. Fortune 500 CEOs move around as much as athletes in the NBA. A recent article in the Business section of the Los Angeles Times began with the headline Owners of Playa Vista Project Look to Former Foe Robert F. Maguire. Faced with the defection of DreamWorks SKG, the company owned by Steven Spielberg, Jeffrey Katzenberg and David Geffen, the owners of the giant Playa Vista development in Southern California, announced they would be relying on the man long considered their chief adversary. Playa Vista's public affairs director, in a dramatic turnabout, even by Hollywood standards, was quoted: "We are very excited. We have every confidence and know Maguire Partners are going to do a great job." *You don't have to be nice to people on the way up if you're not coming back down.*

Disney CEO Michael Eisner and DreamWorks Jeffrey Katzenberg aside, top level executives and/or athletes usually don't include acrimony in their buyout packages. It's not even an issue of forgiveness for these titans of industry. It's just a matter of good business.

The Eisner-Katzenberg squabble was an alarmingly public dispute that occurred when Katzenberg, in an earlier defection, left the Disney fold to create DreamWorks SKG with Spielberg and Geffen. The debate between the heir to Walt Disney and his former chief lieutenant focused on the number of millions due Katzenberg for his contributions to such Disney blockbusters as *The Lion King, Hercules,* and *Beauty and the Beast.*

The case will probably be studied in business schools for years to come as an example of bad business. Although numerous lawyers made a bundle on the case, the Eisner-Katzenberg bloodbath left Disney wounded and at the very least, distracted Katzenberg and DreamWorks from their core business. Even their most cynical colleagues must have found it somewhat distasteful to read about a massacre in Kosovo on one page of the morning newspaper and an article on another page about two spoiled white men with hundreds of millions of dollars squabbling over which one would get or give up another two – five hundred million dollars.

If Than Pok, a Cambodian American who lost eight members of his family to the Khmer Rouge, could give up a successful career in America to try to rebuild a country which includes former Khmer Rouge supporters, old Jeffrey logically should have been able to make do with a payoff of a paltry one hundred million dollars. The wounds he suffered at the hands of Disney cannot possibly compare with the death of parents, brothers and sisters.

One was also tempted to confront Mr. Eisner at a shareholder meeting and say "Even if your adversary doesn't deserve royalties on every animated film Disney ever made and/or will make, just bite the bullet and move on. If he doesn't get the money, the lawyers will and in either case, the shareholders are screwed.

Get over yourselves, boys, and get some perspective!"

In the final analysis, I'm convinced forgiveness is a sound business strategy that saves everyone a lot of time and money.

Rule Number 2: Eat everything that is on your plate.

Nothing endears you to a business associate, a new customer in a foreign country, a restaurant owner or your husband's mother like the knowledge that you like the food they've cooked or chosen.

People in foreign countries, whether they come from some village in Nepal or a beach town in Bali, go to great pains to provide their visitors with the best food they have to offer. In China, France and Japan, the preparation of food is not only a matter of art but national pride. In your mother-in-law's house, your enthusiasm for her cooking may be a matter of survival. In a restaurant, a visible lack of enthusiasm for food, particularly if accompanied by belligerence expressed to a waiter, can actually be hazardous to your health.

Careers are made over the dinner table and deals are lost over someone's lukewarm response to ox-tail soup. Unless you truly have an allergy to a particular dish, gobble it down without blinking. Even if you are unsure of the origin of the meaty substance twitching on your plate, don't ask. As the Victorian Matron advised her daughter on her wedding day, "Just close your eyes and think of England."

I offer this advice with great empathy for people who are the least bit squeamish. I come from an area of the world where burned meat and well-buttered potatoes are considered gourmet dishes. My ideal menu features hamburgers, french fries, chocolate cake and Cherry Garcia ice cream. Left to my own devices, I would live on protein, sugar, and an occasional glass of champagne. Fortunately, I am seldom left to my own devices and have therefore seen the joy in the faces of hosts who have watched me eat food that would never pass a Health Department inspection in America.

I've watched my colleague, Aaron Paley, a world traveller and an arts administrator with a cast-iron stomach, devour a deep-fried, fully-feathered sparrow and ask for seconds. When he was six, I saw my son eat unborn baby eels from a salad bar of delicacies I'd happily have bypassed. In recent years, I've watched him chow down on unidentifiable food from street stalls in Indonesia. My good friend, Brian Toman, consumed food so hot in Mae Hong Son restaurants that the cooks came out of the kitchen to watch and applaud. In China our hosts delighted in ordering increasingly exotic and by American standards, bizarre, dishes for him to sample. This was a daunting experience for me, of course, because I also had to join in the fun and eat the same sea slug and duck's feet he was merrily consuming. Curiously, I found that so long as no one told me what I was eating, almost everything tasted good. Not as good as a well-done steak and Cherry Garcia ice cream but good, nonetheless.

In all instances, these "good eaters" were the toast of the town, the hamlet, and the village.

They were invited by strangers to weddings, funerals, and tooth-filing ceremonies. In several countries, I was invited to do business because of the good will they had created.

The lesson to be learned here is that if you do not have an adventurous palate, you should at least travel with people who do. They will open doors others find bolted shut and they will become, in every sense of the title, Good Will Ambassadors for their companies, their countries, their families and you.

There is nothing like sharing food for breaking down barriers and creating friendships. And for creating an environment in which business can be done. The line "Let's do lunch" is more than a Hollywood affectation. It often means that someone is ready to discuss the terms of a business contract. "Doing lunch" works in business, it works in families and it works in international trade.

On the other side of the coin, picky eaters are a pain in the neck. If they're really picky, they're a pain in the ass. Unless you have some medical condition that requires you to avoid certain foods, there's no excuse for being picky outside your own home. Inside my own house, I feel free to indulge my taste for red meat and white bread. Outside my own dining room, I understand that I should cheerfully swallow whatever my hosts put on my plate.

Restaurants fall outside the purview of this rule. If you're paying for a meal, you have a right to expect your food will be reasonably well-prepared and edible. You have the right to send every other dish back to the kitchen if you choose to do so. (Although as a former waitress with some understanding of what happens to the food of cantankerous customers, I wouldn't advise it.)

I also don't think you should make a practice of sniffing at food if someone else is picking up the tab. I certainly wouldn't indulge myself in expressing disdain if my host had made an effort to introduce me to his favorite restaurant and chef. Criticizing someone's favorite chef comes dangerously close to criticizing a meal cooked by someone's mother. It's not a good idea unless you really <u>don't</u> wish to continue socializing or doing business with this person.

Rule Number 3: Always keep your word

The only excuse for not keeping your word should come attached to a Death Certificate. Whether you're a weekend Dad scheduled to take your son to Disneyland or a business that has promised to ship a supply of plastic sink stoppers to a trade show, you must keep your word.

You may get away with tardiness and if you don't have enough money to buy the Mickey Mouse ears your son wants, he'll have to live with his disappointment. There are all sorts of modifications to your pledge that are acceptable but if you said you were going to put in an appearance at the Magic Kingdom, you'd better show up ready to explore Space Mountain. As a parent and as a business person, short of a coma or some more serious ailment, there are no good excuses for not keeping your word.

There are, on the other hand, lots of very good reasons for not *giving* your word. If you think there is even a remote chance you can't get those sink stoppers to the trade show on time, don't promise to do so. If putting more money into the Disney coffers is likely to break your bank (and if you're taking more than one person to the Happiest Place On Earth, it could), promise Little Eddie a free trip to the park. In short, don't make promises you can't keep. The success of someone else's business or the light in a child's eyes is often at stake, neither of which it is moral for you to place in jeopardy.

Over the years I have known many people whose businesses have failed. In all instances, those people who returned to the playing field were people who accepted responsibility for their failures, paid off their debts even when it took them ten years or more to do so, and who, albeit belatedly, *kept their word*. They didn't file a bankruptcy claim and walk away, they didn't tell themselves they'd repay their debts when they struck it rich and they didn't blame their failures on other people. Instead, they sucked in their stomachs, went to work and faced the people they disappointed. Some of their creditors were paid off in painfully slow $25 payments that may have caused more anger than a bankruptcy would have. Those cases may or may not have ended up in court or arbitration. Most people, however, eventually realized they were not dealing with weasels when they received twelve $25 payments promptly on the fifteenth of each month.

The upside of the downside is that people whose word is their bond, people who do make good on their promises however long it takes them to do so, are frequently considered good business risks. Even banks will take a chance on someone that has had a business fail. In point of fact, banks wouldn't do much business if they boycotted all entrepreneurs with business failures on their records. What bankers find interesting is the way people respond to their failures. If they cut and run and ensure the failure of other businesses by leaving them unable to pay their own bills, banks are not likely to fall over themselves to give the villains start up money for a new business. Unless, of course, the villain is named Trump or Milken. The rest of us, however must, take responsibility for our mistakes and sincerely try to make restitution. Bankers and other hard-hearted business people can show surprising flexibility and generosity if we handle our problems in a responsible way.

Touring artists are often horrified when they arrive at a performance site and discover nothing as it was represented to them. Their accommodations are miles away from the theater, the stage on which they're expected to dance is hazardous to their health and much to their surprise, their fee is suddenly tied to attendance.

When the presenter does not keep his word, the artist is put between a rock and a hard place. If the artist does not keep his word and perform, audience members will be disappointed and word will get around that the artist is a flake. No one is likely to know or care if the stage is in good condition, and cancellation may end up hurting the artist more than the presenter. About all the artist can do is go on as he said he would and never deal with that presenter again. He can also caution other artists to avoid that venue and presenter but, this is a bit like spitting in the ocean. It doesn't have much of an impact. There are, unfortunately, more artists looking for performance opportunities than presenters looking for artists. None of which makes it okay to misrepresent, lie or go back on your word.

Every business will experience bad luck, every adult will make mistakes, and no one will leave this earth unscathed. We will all, at some point, unwittingly or unwillingly, hurt or disappoint others. The trick is not to run from it. How we behave and respond to adversity is the only test of character that counts. Bad luck is not an adequate excuse for breaking your word. Artists and athletes and high tech whiz kids that misbehave with newfound fame and fortune and play fast and loose with contracts and commitments are beyond boring. This tells us only that the gods were sleeping when they gave those sorry souls talent. People who lose fame and fortune or never had it in the first place and *still* manage to lead productive lives as good friends, good parents, good lovers, and good citizens are spectacularly interesting. With words as good as gold, they should be in the Hall of Fame of Interesting People and must be revered.

These rules may seem simplistic and irrelevant to your efforts to increase market share and profits but in my experience, it is not the rules you learned at Harvard Business School that will make or break you. It is the lessons you learned from your Grandpa or from some street vender in Mexico City that will mean the difference between a major contract and the door that hits you in the butt on the way out of a potential client's office. Assuming that most of your competitors are talented and have good products (it is a mistake to assume otherwise), it is often the comradeship established over a meal that gives you an edge. It is the people who set aside their disappointments and move on to reach the finish line in record time and it is the people who keep their word, no matter how difficult it is and no matter how long it takes, that go straight to Heaven. Take it from Sister Mary Margaret. <u>She</u> never lies.

Bibliography

Ayres, Patricia. *Thanks But No Banks*. American Women's Economic Development Corporation. 1994.

Bay Area Lawyers for the Arts. *The Art of Deduction*. BALA. 1983

Bright, Lee Reinke. *The Bright Marketing Handbook*. California: Bright Marketing International. 1996.

Cauvier, Denis L. *How to Hire the Right Person*. HRD Press. 1993.

Dent , Gregory L. and Jeffery E. Johnson. *Tax Planning and Preparation Made Easy for The Self Employed*. Wiley, John and Sons, Inc. 1995

Edwards Directory of American Factors. Edwards Research Group. 1994.

Firestone, Marsha and Bernard Fortunoff. *Busy Woman's Guide To Successful Self-Employment*. New York: Independent Learning Network. 1996.

Foundation Grants to Individuals, 11th Edition. The Foundation Center. May 1999.

Gerber, Jerry. *Life Trends: Your Future For the Next 30 Years*. Avon Books. 1991.

Johnson, Barbara L. *Working Whenever You Want: All About Temporary Emloyment*. Englewood Cliffs, New Jersey: Prentice Hall. 1983

Lownes, Millicent G. *The Purple Rose Within: A Woman's Basic Guide for Developing A Business Plan*. A Business of Your Own.

Luther, Judith. *For The Working Artist*. California: California Institute of the Arts. 1986.

McLean, J.W. *Managing A One-Person Business*. Putnam. 1990.

Messman, Carla. *The Art of Filing*. Pragmatic Publications. 1987.

Millano, Carol. *Hers: The Wise Woman's Guide to Starting A Business on $2000 or Less*. Allworth Press. 1997.

Peters, Tom and Robert Waterman. *In Search of Excellence*. Warner Books, Inc. 1988.

Peters, Tom and Nancy Austin. *Thriving On Chaos*. Random House, Inc. 1995.

Ratliffe, Dolores. *Women Entrepreneurs: Networking and Sweet Potato Pie: Creating Capital in the 21st Century.* Corita Communications. Rev. 1997.

Roddick, Anita with Ronald Miller. *Body and Soul: Profits With Principles.* Random House. November 1991.

Savage, Michael. *Don't Let the IRS Destroy Your Small Business: Seventy Six Mistakes To Avoid.* Addison, Wesley Longman, Inc. 1997.

Southern California Edison Economic Business and Development. *Marketing For Growth and Profits.* Boston: Insights Inc. 1996.

Thwaites, Jeanne C. *Starting And Succeeding In Your Own Photography Business.* Writer's Digest Books. 1984.

Striggles, Theodore W. *Fear of Filing: A Beginner's Guide To Tax Preparation and Record Keeping For Artists, Performers, Writers and Free Lance Professionals.* Dodd, Mead. 1984

Thwaites, Jeanne C. *Starting And Succeeding In Your Own Photography Business.* Writer's Digest Books. 1984

Wong, Angi Ma. *Target: The U.S. Asian Market. A Practical Guide to Doing Business.* California: Pacific Heritage Books. 1993.

Zobel, Jan. *Minding Her Own Business: The Self-Employed Woman's Guide to Taxes And Recordkeeping.* Easthill Press. 1998.

RESOURCES

DISCLAIMER

Listings on the following pages were obtained from numerous sources and were determined to be accurate. However, if you are unable to find an Internet site, we suggest you use one of the search engines listed in the "Internet" resource section. If a telephone number and/or address is no longer valid, try calling an affiliate program in your local area.

GRANTS RESOURCES-BOOKS

The following lists of books contain information on grants, work opportunities, financial aid, awards, etc. If the price of the book was known, it is printed with the title. For prices on the others, please check with the publisher. Note, most of these books can be found in libraries, community foundations, and other nonprofit resource centers.

TITLE	DESCRIPTION	PUBLISHER - DISTRIBUTORS ADDRESS
Arts Funding: An Update on Foundation Trends 3rd Edition $19.95	Provides a framework for understanding recent trends in foundation support for arts and culture.	The Foundation Center 79 Fifth Avenue New York, NY 10003 11/98 69 pp. Order Code ART3
Arts Money: Raising It, Saving It, and Earning It Joan Jeffri, Minneapolis, MN	Traditional funding from private, public and corporate sources or earning it by sharing costs and activities.	University of Minnesota Press, 1989 293 pp. Reference Foundation Collection NX700. J4 1989
Arts, Culture & the Humanities $75.00	Grants to arts and cultural organizations, historic societies and historic preservation, media, visual arts, performing arts, music, and museums.	The Foundation Center 79 Fifth Avenue New York, NY 10003 452 pp. (AC98)
Film, Media & Communications $75.00	Grants for film, video, documentaries, radio, television, printing, publishing, and censorship issues.	The Foundation Center 79 Fifth Avenue New York, NY 10003 136 pp. (FM98)
Foundation Grants for Individuals 11th Edition $65.00	Over 3800 entries paced with the current information that individual grantseekers need most.	The Foundation Center 79 Fifth Avenue New York, NY 10003 5/99 630 pp. Order Code GTI11
Free Money for People in the Arts Laurie Blum, New York, NY	Organizations that provide grants, awards, residency programs, and other means of support for individual artists.	MacMillan, 1991 258 pp. Reference Foundation Collection NX398 .B58 1991

TITLE	DESCRIPTION	PUBLISHER - DISTRIBUTORS ADDRESS
Guide to the National Endowment for the Arts	Publications available from the NEA on arts features, grants given, interviews, etc. (See Internet Resource for website)	National Endowment for the Arts Public Information Office 1100 Pennsylvania Avenue NW Washington, DC 20506
Guide to Women's Art Organizations and Directory for the Arts Cynthia Navaretta New York, NY	Information on visual and performing arts, crafts, writing, film. Contains financial help, emergency funds, and artists' colonies, studying abroad, grants and awards.	Midmarch Associates, 1982 174 pp. Fine Arts Library, 4 West, NX504 .G84 1982
Money Business: Grants and Awards for Creative Artists Rita K. Roosevelt, Anita M. Granoff, and Karen P.F. Kennedy Boston, MA	Directory of organizations that offers financial assistance to poets, fiction writers, playwrights, filmmakers, video artists, composers, choreographers, painters, printmaker's sculptors, craftsmen and photographers.	The Artists Foundation, Inc., 1982 140 pp. Reference Foundation Collection NS397 .R66 1982
Money for Artists: A Guide to Grants and Awards for Individual Artists Laura R. Green, ed. New York, NY	Profiles organizations, government agencies that provide financial support to artists including literary arts, media arts, performing arts, and visual arts.	American Council for the Arts, 1987 241 pp. Reference Foundation Collection NX398 .M66 1987
Money for Visual Artists Douglas Oxenhorn, ed. New York, NY	A guide to grants, awards, fellowships, loan programs; type of award and/or service, eligibility requirements and application procedures.	American Council for the Arts, 1993 2nd edition, 241 pp. Reference Foundation Collection N347 .M59 1993
Money to Work: Grants for Visual Artists, Washington, DC	Provides complete information on fellowships and grants for visual artist working in the U.S.	Art Resources International, 1988 107pp. Reference Foundation Collection N347 .M6 1988
National Directory of Arts and Education Support by Business Corporations Nancy A. Fandell Des Moines, IA	Lists over 600 businesses and corporations who support non-profit arts organizations and those who support individual artists directly.	Arts Letter, 1988 3rd edition, 150 pp. Reference Foundation Collection NX398 .G7

TITLE	DESCRIPTION	PUBLISHER - DISTRIBUTORS ADDRESS
National Directory of Grantmaking Public Charities 2nd Edition $115	Gives grantseekers easy reference to potential sources of funding.	The Foundation Center 79 Fifth Avenue New York, NY 10003 7/98 351 pp. Order Code DGPC2
National Guide to Funding in Arts and Culture 5th Edition $145	5200 Foundations and corporate direct-giving programs, and public charities, each with a history of awarding grant dollars to arts and culture-related projects and organizations.	The Foundation Center 79 Fifth Avenue New York, NY 10003 5/98 1,280 pp. Order Code ARTS5
Whole Arts Directory Cynthia Navarette, New York, NY	Contains information on sources of financial help, artists' colonies, etc.	Midmarch Art Books, 1987 174 pp. Fine Arts Library, 4 West, NX110 .N38 1987

BOOKS/INTERNET SITES

TITLE/SITE NAME	ADDRESS/WEBSITE	NOTES

GRANTS – INTERNET RESOURCES

There are many Internet sites devoted to Grants for Individuals. As you visit any one of them, you'll find links to other Grant sites. As stated in the chapter "The Grantsmanship Game", finding a grant for your project or program requires detailed preparation. When sending a proposal to a private foundation, you must match the foundation's stated mission and priorities. The following list of Internet sites contains a variety of information useful to grantseekers. Some of these sites are fee based.

SITE NAME	DESCRIPTION	INTERNET SITE
The Foundation Center	Guide to foundation grants for individuals	http://www.fdncenter.org
Artsedge Funding Resources Directory	List of organizations which provide funding opportunities and/or resources	http://artsedge. kennedy-center.org/nb/funding/index.
Federal Money Retriever	Federal government funding for Culture/Arts/ Humanities applicants	http://www.idimagic.com/ht mls/grants/ap000007.htm
Cooperating Collections	Free funding information centers by city/communities	http://www.fdncenter.org/col lections/index.
Academy of American Poets	Support for American Poets at all stages of their careers	http://www.poets.org/aap/aap frmst.htm
Arts and Humanities Update	Arts and humanities award information from COS Funding Opportunities	http://fundingopps2.cos.com/ news/humanities
Arts Wire	Provides directory of arts organizations that may provide assistance	http://www.artswire.org/Arts wire/www/ current.html#money
Creative Arts and Humanities Report	Up-to-date information on funding opportunities and policies in the creative arts and humanities	http://www.lib.msu.edu/harri s23/grants/ariscart.htm
Dactyl Foundation for the Arts and Humanities	Not-for-profit organization that offers a $3,000 award for essays	http://www.dactyl.org
Foundations, Grants and Trusts: A Comprehensive Resource for Sculptors	Collection of links and descriptions or organizations which fund sculptors.	http://www.sculptor.org/fund ing.htm
Guide to Funding: A Reference Directory to Public and Private Giving for Artists/Scholars	Compiled by the President's Committee on the Arts and Humanities	http://www.amherst.edu/~err eich/pcah_html/fundingguide .html

SITE NAME	DESCRIPTION	INTERNET SITE
Lila Wallace-Reader's Digest Fund	Mission to invest in programs that enhance the cultural life of communities	http://www.lilawallace.org
National Foundation for the Advancement of the Arts	Mission is to support exceptional young artists with cash awards	http://www.nfaa.org
National Initiative to Preserve America's Dance Grants Program	Sponsored by the Kennedy Center	http://save-as-dance.org91/nipad/html/apply.html
Poets and Writers Magazine Grants and Awards Page	Compilation of resources by the editors	http://www.pw.org/mag/grantsawards.htm
Women's Studio Workshop	Opportunities for visual artists in state of art printmaking, papermaking & photography	http://www.wsworkshop.org/
World Wide Art Resources	Site offers funding and contact information for arts organizations all over the world	http://wwar.com/
American Library Association	Internet resources for grants and foundations	http://www.ala.org/acrl/resmay97.html
Yahoo's Lists of Arts Foundations	Foundations that provide assistance to individuals	http://www.yahoo.com/Arts/Organizations/Foundations
Community Resource Institute's Grant Funding Resource	Foundations with Arts and Cultural Funding	http://www.granted.org/artculture.html
Pacific Bell's Grant Opportunity Resources	Access to grant information and resources available on line	http://www.kn.pacbell.com/wired/grants/locate.htm
SRA's Grantsweb	Starting point for accessing grants-related information and resources.	http://web.fie.com/cws/sra/resource.htm
Opportunities Gateways	An index of funding resources on the Getty Center's ArtsEdNet site.	http://artsdnet.getty.edu/ArtsEdNet/Gateways/opportun.html
Artists Space	Grants distributed to individual arts and groups of artists on a lottery basis – including visual arts, film & video, new medial and performance pieces.	http://www.artistsspace,org/indep_project.html
MMAAC Grant Opportunities	Grant program designed to support emerging media artists and foster diversity in media arts.	http://www.mtn.org/MMAAC/grant.html

MICROLENDERS

The Association for *Entrepreneurial Opportunity,* is a program that provides a variety of services from lending to technical assistance and training for for entrepreneurs. Call 800 827-5722 for more information about AEO microloan programs. Call the office in your area to find out about specific programs they offer. For a copy of the original list of Microloan Intermediaries call ASBA at 800 272-2911.

NAME	ORGANIZATION	ADDRESS	CITY	STATE	ZIP CODE	TEL/FAX #
Kathryn J. Maieli	Women $ Fund	245 W. 5th Avenue P.O. Box 102059	Anchorage	AK	99510-2059	907-274-1524 907-272-3146
Charles Northrip	Juneau Economic Development Council Microenterprise Program	612 W. Willoughby Ave. Suite A	Juneau	AK	99801	907-463-3662 907-463-3929
Bonnie Savland	Central Council of Tlingit and Haida Indian Tribes of AK	320 W, Willoughby Ave. Suite 300	Juneau	AK	99801-1789	907 463-7121 907 463-7316
Robert Dickerson	Birmingham Business Resource Center	110 12th Street No.	Birmingham	AL	35203	205 250-6380 205 2506384
Barbara Royal	YWCA of Birmingham	309 North 23rd Street	Birmingham	AL	35203	205 322-9922
Charles M. Stockton	FORGE, Inc.	P.O. Box 1138	Huntsville	AR	72740-1138	501-738-1585 501-738-6288
Penny Penrose	Arkansas Enterprise Group	2304 W. 29th	Pine Bluff	AR	71603	870-535-6233 870-535-0741
Lisa Borstadt	Northern Arizona Small Business Loan Fund	1300 South Milton Road Suite 125	Flagstaff	AZ	86001	520-226-9525 520-226-9526
Jean Rosenberg	Self Employment Loan Fund, Inc. (SELF)	201 N. Central Avenue Suite CC10	Phoenix	AZ	85073-1000	602-340-8834 602-340-8953
Frank Ballesteros	PMHDC Micro	1100 E. Ajo Way Suite 209	Tucson	AZ	85713	520-806-9513 520-806-9515
James I. Masters	Center for Community Futures	P.O. Box 5309	Berkeley	CA	94705	510-339-3801 510-339-3803
Faye McNair-Knox	Start Up	1935 University Avenue Suite A	East Palo Alto	CA	94303	650 321-2193 650 321-1025
Tou Xiong	Economic Opportunities Commission	1900 Mariposa Mall #111	Fresno	CA	93721	559-263-1290 559-263-1549
Richard S. Amador	CHARO Community Development Corporation	3951 E. Medford Street	Los Angeles	CA	90063-1698	323-269-0751 323-266-4326
Menelva Boyd	Community Financial Resource Center	4060 S. Figueroa Street	Los Angeles	CA	90037	323 233-1900 323 235-1686
Forescee Hogan-Rowles	Community Financial Resource Center	4060 S. Figueroa Street	Los Angeles	CA	90037	323 233-1900 323 235-1686
Ana Rubalcaba	Community Financial Resource Center	4060 S. Figueroa Street	Los Angeles	CA	90037	323 233-1900 323 235-1686
Mari Riddle	Los Angeles Community Development Bank	5312 S. Vermont Avenue	Los Angeles	CA	90037	323 759-7759 ext. 117 323 759-7750

NAME	ORGANIZATION	ADDRESS	CITY	STATE	ZIP CODE	TEL/FAX #
Nancy Swift	The Development Resource	P.O. Box 1193	Mt. Shasta	CA	96067	530-926-6255 530-926-1021
Stephen Walsh	Berkeley Planning Associates	440 Grand Avenue Suite 500	Oakland	CA	94610-5085	510-465-7884 510-465-7885
Catherine Marshall	CAMEO - California Association for Microenterprise Opportunity	655 13th Street Suite 201	Oakland	CA	94612	510-238-8360 510-238-8361
Cheral Stewart	YWCA of the Mid-Peninsula	4161 Alma Street	Palo Alto	CA	94306-4546	650-494-0972 650-494-8307
Betty Futrell	Microenterprise Assistance Program SCEDD	1003 Yuba Street	Redding	CA	96002	530-225-2780 530-225-2779
Maurine Huang	Microenterprise Assistance Program	2117 Cottage Way	Sacramento	CA	95825	916-568-5020 916-568-7268
Diana Douglas	Sacramento Employment and Training Agency (SETA)	1217 Del Paso Blvd.	Sacramento	CA	95815	916 263-4607
Sandra Brown	Sacramento Employment and Training Agency (SETA)	1217 Del Paso Blvd.	Sacramento	CA	95815	916 263-4607
Jennifer Vanica	Jacobs Center for Non-Profit Innovation	P.O. Box 740650	San Diego	CA	92174-0650	619-527-6161 619-527-6162
Velma Landers	Prince Hall Apartments	1170 McAllister Suite 405	San Francisco	CA	94115	415 922-2773 415 922-5391
Barbara Johnson	Women's Initiative for Self Employment (WISE)	450 Mission Street Suite 402	San Francisco	CA	94109	415-247-9473 415-247-9471
Marsha Bailey	Women's Economic Ventures of Santa Barbara	1136 E. Montecito Street	Santa Barbara	CA	93103	805-965-6073 805-962-9622
Sheilah Rogers	West Company	367 N. State Street Suite 201	Ukiah	CA	95482	707-468-3559 707-468-3555
Bill Bridges	Belay Enterprises, Inc.	1530 Marion Street	Denver	CO	80217	303-894-9495 303-839-5241
Gregory Cooke	Colorado Capital Initiatives	1616 17th Street Suite 371	Denver	CO	80202	303-628-5464 303-628-5469
Cameron Wold	Colorado Center for Community Development	P.O. Box 173364 Campus Box 128	Denver	CO	80217-3364	303-620-4666 303-620-4670
Tamela Lee	Denver Small Business Development Center	1445 Market Street	Denver	CO	80202-1729	303-620-8076 303-534-3200
Ceyl Prinster	Colorado Enterprise Fund	1888 Sherman Street Suite 530	Denver	CO	80203-1159	303-860-0242 303-860-0409
Gerald Moore	Bridgeport Artisan Center	955 Connecticut Ave Suite 1215	Bridgeport	CT	06607	203 382-5440 203 382-5442
Jean Blake-Jackson	Hartford College Entrepreneurial Center	50 Elizabeth Street	Hartford	CT	06105-2280	860 768-5681 860 768-5622
Alyce Hild	Loaves and Fishes Ministries, Inc.	120 Sigourney Street	Hartford	CT	06105-2796	860 524-1730 860 249-2871
Barbara Potopowitz	Permanent Commission on the Status of Women	18-20 Trinity Street	Hartford	CT	06106	860 240-8300 860 240-8314
Shellina White	Livable Income for Everyone LIFE	c/o CCA 169 Davenport Ave	New Haven	CT	06519	203 777-7848 203 777-7923

NAME	ORGANIZATION	ADDRESS	CITY	STATE	ZIP CODE	TEL/FAX #
Fran Pastore	Women's Development Center	400 Main Street	Stamford	CT	06901	203 353-1750 203 353-1084
Patricia Woolwich	Access Agency, Inc.	1315 Main Street	Willimantic	CT	06226	860 450-7146 860 450-7477
Cristina Himes	ACCION International	733 15th Street, N. W. 7th Floor	Washington	DC	20005-2112	202 393-5113 202 393-5115
Patsy Fletcher	Barry Farm Res. Council	1326 Stevens Rd SE	Washington	DC	20020	202 645-3854 202 889-2340
Michael Barr	Community Development Policy	1500 Pennsylvania Avenue, NW	Washington	DC	20220	202 622-0016 202 622-5672
Karen Sherman	Counterpart International	1200 18th Street, NW Suite 1100	Washington	DC	20036	202 296-9676 202 296-9679
Lawrence Yanovitch	FINCA Foundation for International Community Assistance	1101 14th Street NW, 11th Floor	Washington	DC	20005-5601	202 682-1510 202 682-1535
Donald L. Hense	Friendship House Association, Inc.	619 D Street SE	Washington	DC	20003	202 675-9050 202 546-3080
Alex Counts	Grameen Foundation USA	1709 New York Ave. NW Suite 101	Washington	DC	20006	202 628-3560 202 628-3880
William Barrow	H Street Community Development Corporation	501 H Street NE	Washington	DC	20002	202 544-8353 202 544-3051
Caroline Glackin	First State Community Loan Fund	100 W. 10th Street Suite 1005	Wilmington	DE	19801	302 652-6774 302 656-1272
Mary Dupont	YWCA Working Capital/Delaware	233 King Street	Wilmington	DE	19801	302 658-7161 302 658-7547
Gerald O. Chester	Central Florida Community Development Corporation, Inc.	P.O. Box 15065	Daytona Beach	FL	32115	904 258-7520 904 238-3428
Florina Hepburn	Hepburn Rental Services, Inc.	P.O. Box 254	Hallandale	FL	33008	954 454-7429 954 456-8450
Valerie Williams	First Coast Micro Program, Inc.	5923 Norwood Avenue	Jacksonville	FL	32208	904 924-1100 904 924-1103
Diane Reeves	Florida WWINS	P.O. Box 4277	Tallahasse	FL	32315	561 881-9212 561 881-9217
Dan Horvath	Community Equity Investments, Inc.	302 N. Barcelona St	Pensacola	FL	32501	850 595-6234 850 595-6264
Marilyn Kershner	Florida Community Loan Fund, Inc.	8601 4th St. North #305D	St. Petersburg	FL	33702-3116	813 578-2030 813 578-5609
Kathy Keeley	Atlanta Microfund	3137 Bolero Pass	Atlanta	GA	30341	770 939-2443 770 938-9358
Diana Moore	Center for Black Women's Wellness	477 Windsor Street SW Suite 309	Atlanta	GA	30312	404 688-9202 404 880-9435
Elizabeth Williams	Goodwill Industries Business NOW	2201 Glenwood Ave SE	Atlanta	GA	30316	404 486-8452 404 377-0754
Chris Martin	Quality Care For Children Inc.	1447 Peachtree Street, Suite 700	Atlanta	GA	30309-3030	404 479-4200 404 479-4166
Cheryl Desbordes	Working Capital Atlanta	60 Walton Street 4th Floor	Atlanta	GA	30303	404 688-6884 404 688-4009

NAME	ORGANIZATION	ADDRESS	CITY	STATE	ZIP CODE	TEL/FAX #
Patricia Harris	Cobb Microenterprise Council Kennesaw State University Small Business Development Center	1000 Chastain Rd – BB423	Kennesaw	GA	30144	770 499-3228 770 423-6564
Nancy Shah	Big Island Sustainable Community Association	111 East Puainako Street Suite 405	Hilo	HI	96720-0847	808-935-0229 808-961-9000
Patricia K. Brandt	Hawaii Community Loan Fund	680 Iwilei Road Suite 665	Honolulu	HI	96817-5388	808-523-0075 808-534-1199
Christine Van Bergeijk	Office of Hawaiian Affairs	711 Kapiolani Blvd. Suite 500	Honolulu	HI	96813	808-594-1927 808-594-1865
Tin Myaing Thein Ph.D.	The Immigrant Center	720 N. King Street	Honolulu	HI	96817	808-845-3918 808-842-1962
Mel Higa	Kahuku Federal Credit Union	P.O. Box 245	Kahuku	HI	96731	808 293-9063 808 293-7667
David Lawrence	Maui Economic Opportunity Inc.	P.O. Box 2122	Kahului	HI	96733-2122	808 871-9591 808 871-2426
Joseph Lapilio	Queen Liliuokalani Children's Center	87-1876 Farrington Highway	Waianae	HI	96792	808-668-2314 808-668-8811
Cheryl De La Cruz	Waianae Court Coalition/ Waianae Business Center	85-670 Farrington Highway Suite 1	Waianae	HI	96792	808 696-1217 808 696-5217
Jason Friedman	Institute for Social and Economic Development	1901 Broadway Suite 313	Iowa City	IA	52240	319 338-2331 319 338-5824
Carmen Jimenez	ACCION Chicago	3245 W. 26th St. 2nd Floor	Chicago	IL	60623-4034	773 376-9004 773 376-9048
Steve McCullough	CANDO-Chicago Association of Neighborhood Development Organization	123 West Madison Suite 1100	Chicago	IL	60602-4589	312 372-2636 312 372-2637
Debra L. Osborn	Community Economic Development Law Project	188 West Randolph Suite 2103	Chicago	IL	60601	312 939-3638 312 427-6172
Hazel King	Illinois Institute for Entrepreneur Education	62 W. Huron Street 2nd Floor	Chicago	IL	60610	312 587-9296 312 587-9483
Wil Berry	Mid-South Planning & Development Commission	4309 S. King Drive	Chicago	IL	60653	773 924-1330 773 924-3151
Scott Parrott	National Institute for Social Science Information	P.O. Box 11203	Chicago	IL	60611	312 988-6589 312 988-6579
Eden Hurd	Faith Corp Fund	2929 South Wabash, STE 200	Chicago	IL	60616	312-674-2337 312-674-0551
Carol Petersen	The Salvation Army	1515 W. Monroe	Chicago	IL	60607	312 733-2533 312 733-5138
Curtis Roeschley	Uptown Center Hull House Economic Development Unit	4520 N. Beacon	Chicago	IL	60640-5519	773 561-3500 773 561-3507
Mary Anne Angle	Women's Business Development Center	8 South Michigan Ave. Suite 400	Chicago	IL	60603	312 853-3477 312 853-0145

NAME	ORGANIZATION	ADDRESS	CITY	STATE	ZIP CODE	TEL/FAX #
Connie E. Evans	Women's Self Employment Project	20 N.Clark Suite 400	Chicago	IL	60602	312 606-8255 312 606-9215
Carlos Ray	World Relief Chicago	3507 W. Lawrence Avenue Suite 208	Chicago	IL	60625	773 583-9191 773 583-9410
Javier Placencia	Elgin Community College	1700 Spartan Drive	Elgin	IL	60123-7193	847 697-1000
Max E. Baumgardner	Tri-County Opportunities Council c/o M.E. Baumgardner Associates	8986 So. Lowden Rd	Franklin Grove	IL	61031	815 456-2083
Linda M. Jorn	Small Business Development Center College of Lake County	19351 W. Washington St.	Grayslake	IL	60030	847 223-6601 847 223-9371
Thomas C. Coleman	Microenterprise Finance Consulting	624 Lakeside Dr.	Hinsdale	IL	60521	630 986-5166
Thomas S. Ullmann	Micro Works	325 Oxford Road	Kenilworth	IL	60043-1101	847 853-9401 847 853-9439
Margaret Walen	Opportunity International	2122 York Rd. #340	Oak Brook	IL	60523-1930	630 645-4600 630 645-1458
Larry Golden	University of Illinois @ Springfield	P.O. Box 19243, PAC 363	Springfield	IL	62794-9243	217 206-7819 217 206-6542
Michael A. McMahon	West Cook Community Development Corp.	1127 S. Mannheim Rd. Suite 102	Westchester	IL	60514	708 450-0100 708 450-0655
Leigh Sahiduny	Community Action of Southern Indiana	1613 East 8th Street	Jeffersonville	IN	47131	812 288-6451 812 284-8314
Linda Gilkerson	Neighborhood Self-Employment Initiative	P.O. Box 2927	Indianapolis	IN	46206	317 631-5430 317 631-5430
Earnesto Pae	LaCasa of Goshen, Inc.	202 N. Cottage Avenue	Goshen	IN	46528	219-533-4450 219-553-4399
Carol A. Peak	Kansas Center for Rural Initiatives	8D Edwards Hall Kansas State University	Manhattan	KS	66506-4805	785 532-0672 785 532-0671
Terri Petri	Women Vision International	6405 Metcalf Suite 509	Overland Park	KS	66202	913 432-2883 913 341-9796
Debbie Beck	Kansas Department of Commerce & Housing	700 SW Harrison Suite 1300	Topeka	KS	66603	785 296-3004 785 296-0186
Gary Satter	Glacial Hills Small Business Development Program	318 Broadway	Valley Falls	KS	66088-1302	785 945-6292 785 945-6882
John Allard	Bowling Green Housing Authority	247 Double Springs Road	Bowling Green	KY	42101	502 843-6071 502 781-7091
Jipaum Askew-Gibson	South Central Kentucky Minority Economic Development Council	P.O. Box 90005	Bowling Green	KY	42102-9005	502 781-2381 502 842-0768
Kevin Smith	Community Ventures Corporation	1450 N. Broadway	Lexington	KY	40505-3162	606 231-0054 606 231-0261
Brenda McDaniel	Kentucky Highlands Investment Corp.	362 Old Whitley Rd	London	KY	40743	606 864-5175 606 864-5194
Robert Heil	Jewish Family & Vocational Services	3640 Dutchmans Lane	Louisville	KY	40205-3276	502 452-6341 502 452-6718

NAME	ORGANIZATION	ADDRESS	CITY	STATE	ZIP CODE	TEL/FAX #
Sam Watkins	Louisville Central Development Corporation	1015 W. Chestnut Street	Louisville	KY	40203	502 589-1173 509 583-8824
Claudia Saucier	Coastal Entrepreneurials Net to Success	1220 Aycosk Street P.O. Box 3894	Houma	LA	70360	504-876-0490 504-876-7751
Paul Dunn	SBDC NE LA University	700 University Avenue ADM 2-123	Monroe	LA	71209	318-342-1224 318-342-1209
Monica Johnson	New Orleans Jazz and Heritage Foundation	1205 North Rampart St.	New Orleans	LA	70116	504-522-4786 504-558-6148
Andrea Silbert	Center for Women and Enterprise Inc.	1135 Tremont Street Suite 480	Boston	MA	02120	617 423-3001 617 423-2444
Nikki Fliones	Creating Value Enterprises	17 Hemingway Suite 1	Boston	MA	02115	617 266-5084
Joseph Kriesberg	Massachusetts Association of CDC's	99 Chauncy Street Fifth Floor	Boston	MA	02111	617 426-0303 617 426-0344
Paula Zayas Planthaber	Neighborhood Reinvestment Corp	607 Boylston 5th Floor	Boston	MA	02116	617 450-0420 617 450-0424
Barbara Rosenbaum	Jewish Vocational Service, Inc.	105 Chauncy, 6th FLR	Boston	MA	02111	617-451-8147 617-451-9973
Ameeta Alter	Women's Educational and Industrial Union (WEIU)	356 Boylston Street	Boston	MA	02116	617-536-5651 617-247-8826
Peg Barringer	OKM Association Inc.	164 Canal Street	Boston	MA	02114	617 742-8616 617 742-1069
Jorgette Theophilis	Women's Institute for Housing & Economic Development	14 Beacon Street Suite 608	Boston	MA	02801	617 367-0520 617-367-1676
Barry Dicker,	Barry M. Dicker, Attorney at Law	872 Massachusetts Ave Suite 1-6	Cambridge	MA	02139-3013	617 576-9990 617 576-9991
Priscilla Caouette	Hilltown Comm. Dev. Corp.	432A Main Road	Chesterfield	MA	01012-0017	413 296-4536 413-296-4020
Susan Worgaftik	DCAE	269 E. Cottage Street	Dorchester	MA	02130	
Glen Prospere	Christian Economic Coalition	493 Washington Street	Dorchester	MA	02124	617-929-0352 617-288-7788
Jeanne A. DuBois	Dorchester Bay Economic Development Corp.	594 Columbia Rd. Suite 302	Dorchester	MA	02125	617 825-4200 617 825-3522
Betsy Hannula	Twin Cities Community Development Corp.	195 Kimball Street	Fitchburg	MA	01420	978 342-9561 978 345-7905
Emily Kearns	Community Action, Inc.	25 Locust Street	Haverhill	MA	01832	508-373-1971 508-373-8966
Christopher Sikes	Western Mass. Development Fund Inc.	308 Main Street Suite 2B	Greenfield	MA	01301-3201	413 774-4033 413 774-3673
Tom Giossi	Lowell Small Business Assistance Center	169 Merrimack Street, 3rd FLR	Lowell	MA	01852	978-441-1889 978-441-6824
James Canavan	Community Teamwork, Inc.	167 Dutton Street	Lowell	MA	01852	978-459-0551 978-453-9128
Julie A. Early	Island Foundation, Inc.	589 Mill Street	Marion	MA	02738-1553	508 748-2809 508 748-0991

NAME	ORGANIZATION	ADDRESS	CITY	STATE	ZIP CODE	TEL/FAX #
Bill Maddocks	Community Economic Development Center Of SE MA	105 William Street	New Bedford	MA	02742	508 979-4684 508 990-0199
Maria Gooch-Smith	South Eastern Economic Development Corporation	88 Broadway	Taunton	MA	02780	508-822-1020 508-880-7869
James Asselin	Springfield Business Development Fund	1176 Main Street	Springfield	MA	01103	413 781-6900 413 736-0650
Peter Radzinski	Center for Business Work and Learning/ The Enterprise Center (CBWL)	226 Lowell Street Suite B6	Wilmington	MA	01887	508 988-2118 508 988-2128
Jacquelyn D. Cornish	Druid Heights Community Development Corp.	1821 McCulloh Street	Baltimore	MD	21217	410 523-1350 410 523-1374
Paula Klepper	Mid-Atlantic Business Finance Company	1410 Crain Highway, STE 5B	Baltimore	MD	21225	410 863-1600 410 863-7446
Rosemarie Lazzati	Maryland Capitol Enterprise Inc.	428 Pinehurst Avenue	Salisburg	MD	21801	410 548-9778 410 548-4995
Denise Graves	Johns Hopkins University	808 North Chester Street	Baltimore	MD	21205	410-614-4216 410 614-9438
Stephen McHenry	Forum for Rural Maryland	219 East Redwood Street, 10th FLR	Baltimore	MD	21202	410-767-6518 410-333-8314
Amanda Crook Zinn	Women Entrepreneurs of Baltimore	1118 Light St.#202	Baltimore	MD	21230-4105	410 727-4921 410 727-4989
Elizabeth Collins	GMS, Inc.	10559 Metropolitan Ave.	Kensington	MD	20895	800 933-3501 301 933-3502
Helen Spinelli	Caroline County Department of Economic Development	16 North 2nd Street	Denton	MD	21629	410-479-1063 410-479-4061
Mikal R. McCartney	Garrett Count Community Action Committee	104 E. Center Street	Oakland	MD	21550	301 334-9431 301 334-8555
Eloise Vitelli	Maine Centers for Women, Work & Community	46 University Drive Stoddard House, UMA	Augusta	ME	04330-9410	207 621-3432 207 621-3429
Gilda E. Nardone	Maine Centers for Women, Work & Community	46 University Drive	Augusta	ME	04330-9410	207 621-3437 207 621-3429
Stephen R. Duval	Maine Workforce Development Center.	124 State House Station Hospital Street	Augusta	ME	04333	207 287-3378 207 287-3611
Debbie N. Metzler	Eastern Maine Development Corp.	One Cumberland Place STE 300	Bangor	ME	04401	207 942-6389 207 942-3548
Sandra K. Prescott	Washington-Hancock Community Agency	Corner of Maple & Main Street PO Box 280	Milbridge	ME	04658-0280	207 546-7544 207 546-3216
Diane Hutchinson	MaineSpring	PO Box 554	Portland	ME	04102-0554	207 655-3662 207 655-5330
Jeffrey Heron	Aroostook County Action Program, Inc.	18 Dyer Street	Presque Isle	ME	04769	207 768-3033 207 768-3040
Ellen F. Golden	Coastal Enterprises, Inc. (CEI)	P.O. Box 268	Wiscasset	ME	04578	207 882-7552 207 882-7308
Cathy McClelland	Detroit Entrepreneurship Institute, Inc.	455 W. Fort Street 4th Floor	Detroit	MI	48226	313 961-8426 313 961-8831

NAME	ORGANIZATION	ADDRESS	CITY	STATE	ZIP CODE	TEL/FAX #
Bobby J. Wells	Community Capital Development Corporation	711 N. Saginaw St. #102	Flint	MI	48503-1703	810 239-4857 810 239-5575
Paula Brush	GROW	25 Sheldon Street SE Suite 210	Grand Rapids	MI	49503	616 458-3404 616 458-6557
Rebekah Fennel	Healthy Futures	1000 Oakland Drive	Kalamazoo	MI	49008-1284	616 337-4440 617 337-4234
Todd Horton	Northern Initiatives	228 W. Washington	Marquette	MI	49855	907 228-5571 906 228-5572
Madonna May	Northwest Michigan Council of Governments	2194 Dendrinos Drive	Traverse City	MI	49685	231 929-5028 231 929-5012
Steve Schnoeneck	NW Minnesota Initiative Fund	4225 Technology Dr. NW	Bemidji	MN	56601	218 759-2057 218 759-2328
Frank Altman	Community Reinvestment Fund	2400 Foshay Tower 821 Marquette Avenue	Minneapolis	MN	55402	612 338-3050 612 338-3236
Betty C. Mosley	Institute for Applied Community Economic Development	4830 Oakland Avenue South	Minneapolis	MN	55417	612 823-5193 612 823-3396
John Baker	Arrowhead Community Economic Assistance Corp.	8880 Main Street	Mountain Iron	MN	55768-0406	218 735-8201 218 735-8202
Mihalio Temali	Neighborhood Development Center, Inc.	651 ½ University Avenue	S. Paul	MN	55104	612 291-2480 612 291-2597
Peggy Metzer	Women Venture	2324 University Avenue Suite 200	St. Paul	MN	55114	612 646-3808 612 641-7223
John Pegg	North Star Community Development Corporation	301 West First Street	Deluth	MN	55802-1613	218-727-6690 218-723-7120
Mary Mathews	Northeast Entrepreneur Fund, Inc.	Olcott Plaza 820 Ninth Street, North Ste 200	Virginia	MN	55792	218 749-4191 218 749-5213
Tina Sterling	Rural Missouri Inc.	1014 Northeast Drive	Jefferson City	MO	65109-2504	573 635-0136 573 635-5636
Stephanie Weaver	Kauffman Center	4900 Oak Street	Kansas City	MO	64112	816 932-1000 816 932-1420
Vanessa Finley	The First Step Fund	1080 Washington Street Suite 204	Kansas City	MO	64105-2216	816 474-5111 816 472-4207
Jane Vanderham	Thomas Hill Enterprise Center	1709 Prospect Drive	Macon	MO	63552	660 385-6550 660 385-6568
Jan Hureke	International Institute of St. Louis	3800 Park Avenue	St. Louis	MO	63110	314 773-9090 314 773-6047
Betsy Slosar	Missouri Association for Social Welfare	621 Lee Avenue	St. Louis	MO	63119	314 963-9227 314 963-9809
Michael Sherraden	Washington University	Campus Box 1196 One Brooking Drive	St. Louis	MO	63130-4899	314 935-7433 314 935-8661
Mike Spady	Historic Northeast Restoration Corp.	6612 Independence Avenue	Kansas City	MO	64151	816-483-9888 816-231-3708
Sister Noel LeClaire	Sacred Heart Southern Missions Economic Alternatives	395 North West Street	Holly Springs	MS	38635	601 252-1575 601 252-6673

NAME	ORGANIZATION	ADDRESS	CITY	STATE	ZIP CODE	TEL/FAX #
Robert L. Jackson	Quitman County Development Organization	201 Humphrey Street	Marks	MS	38646	601 326-4000 601 326-3904
James R. Scott	First Interstate Foundation	611 N. 31st Street	Billings	MT	59103-7113	406 248-8555 406 248-2092
Jeffrey K. Rupp	Human Resource Development Council of District IX	321 E. Main Street Suite 300	Bozeman	MT	59715	406 587-4486 406 585-3538
Robyn Hampton	Montana Department of Commerce Montana Microbusiness Finance	1424 Ninth Avenue	Helena	MT	59620	406 444-4325 406 444-1872
Emily Miller	Small Business Solutions	23 Willowbrook	Missoula	MT	59802-3333	406 542-0066 406 542-5166
Bill Hubbard	East Carolina Microenterprise Fund	2407 Grace Avenue #9	New Bern	NC	28562-4445	252 504-2424 252 504-2248
Michael Atkinson	First Citizens Bank	3127 Smoketree Court	Raleigh	NC	27604	919-716-7282 919-716-2751
Robert Todd	Yadkin Valley Economic Development District	3801 E. River Road	Boonville	NC	27011	910 367-7251 910 367-4395
Phillip Black	North Carolina Rural Economic Development Center	4021 Carya Drive	Raleigh	NC	27610	919-250-4314 919-250-4325
Meena Geraud	Self-Help	801 Baxter Street Suite 410	Charlotte	NC	28202	919-956-4400 919-956-4410
Carolyn A. Prince	The North Carolina Coalition of Farm & Rural Families	342 Wagoner Drive Suite 208	Fayetteville	NC	28303	910 860-9948 910 860-9951
Greg Walker Wilson	Mountain Microenterprise Fund	29 ½ Page Avenue	Asheville	NC	28801	828-253-2834 828-255-7953
Floyd Shorter	Southeastern Community College	Box 151	Whiteville	NC	28472	910-642-7141 910-642-5658
Theresa Roberson	Sandhills Community College	2200 Airport Road	Pinehurst	NC	28374	910-695-3832 910-692-6998
Bob Hobbs	Mid Nebraska Community Services, Inc.	16 W. 11th Street	Kearney	NE	68848-2288	308 865-5675 308 865-5681
Marilyn Schlake	Nebraska Edge Center for Rural Revitalization	University of Nebraska 58 Filley Hall	Lincoln	NE	68583-0947	402 472-4138 402 472-0688
Rick R. Wallace	Lincoln Self-Employment Loan Fund (Self)	1135 M St., 3rd Fl, Ste 116	Lincoln	NE	68508	402 436-2386 402 436-2360
Trine Mc Bride	Central Nebraska Community Services,	P.O Box 509	Loup City	NE	68853-0509	308 745-0780 308 745-0824
Renay Robinson-Scheer	Northeast Nebraska Economic Development District	111 S. First St.	Norfolk	NE	68701	402 379-1150 402 379-9207
Edward Kentch	First National Bank of Omaha	One First National Center 1620 Dodge St., LM11	Omaha	NE	68102-1596	402 633-7405 402 633-7426
Michael B. Maroney	New Community Development Corporation	Redick Professional Plaza 3147 Ames Avenue	Omaha	NE	68111-2760	402 451-2939 402 451-2595

NAME	ORGANIZATION	ADDRESS	CITY	STATE	ZIP CODE	TEL/FAX #
Nariman Ajluni	Catholic Charities- San Juan Diego Center	5211 S. 31st Street	Omaha	NE	68107	402 731-5413 402 721-5865
Barb Baier	Lincoln Action Program, Inc.	2202 S. 11th St.	Lincoln	NE	68502	402 471-4515, x230;
Nanette Shackleford	Center For Research & Development	Welch Hall- U. of Neb/Kearney, 19th & Univ. Drive	Kearney	NE	68849-4441	402 762-3648 308 865-8153
Eugene Severens	NEON Partnership	RR 1 Box 34	Rosalie	NE	68055	402-863-2567 402-863-2577
Kendall Scheer	REAP, Center for Rural Affairs	101 S. Tallman, P.O. Box 406	Walthill	NE	68067	402 846-5428 402 846-5420
Mary Coonan	New Hampshire College-CED Program	2500 North River Rd.	Manchester	NH	03106-1045	603-644-3103 603-644-3130
Liz Lisk	New Hampshire Community Loan Fund	7 Wall Street	Concord	NH	03301	603-224-6669 603-225-7425
Racheal Stuart	Women's Business Center, Inc.	150 Greenleaf Avenue, #4	Portsmouth	NH	03801	603-430-2892 603-430-3706
Aaron A. Bocage	EDTEC	313 Market St. Suite 302	Camden	NJ	08102	609 342-8277 609 963-8110
Anne S. Li	New Jersey Community Loan Fund	16-18 W. Lafayette St.	Trenton	NJ	08608	609 989-7766 609 393-9401
Irene Stoltzenberg	Jewish Family and Vocational Services of Middlesex	10 Franklin Avenue	Edison	NJ	08830	732 738-5225
Deborah Osgood	Trenton Bus. Asst. Corp. (TBAC)	36 S. Broad St.	Trenton	NJ	08608	609 396-8271 609 396-8603
Rockling Todea	New Mexico Community Development Loan Fund	P.O. Box 705, 115 Second St.	Albuquerque	NM	87103-0705	505-243-3196 505-243-8803
Agnes Noonan	WESST Corporation	414 Silver Avenue SW	Albuquerque	NM	87102-3239	505-241-4758 505-241-4766
Anna Siefert	Nevada Microenterprise Initiative, dba Microenterprise Dev. Corp.	116 East 7th St., Ste 3	Carson City	NV	89701	775 841-1420 775 841-2221
Terry Ludwig	ACCION New York	235 Havemeyer Street, 2nd Floor	Brooklyn	NY	11211	718-599-5170 718-387-9686
Ernest Hohmeyer	Adirondack Economic Development Corporation	Trudeau Road, PO Box 747	Saranac Lake	NY	12983	518-891-5523 518-891-9820
Inger Guiffreda	Alternatives Federal Credit Union	301 West State Street	Ithaca	NY	14850	607-272-1236 607-277-6391
Tony Ebersole	Appleseed Trust	220 Herald Place 2nd Floor	Syracuse	NY	13202	315-424-9485 315-424-7056
Ruth Ellen Simmonds	Associated Blind, Inc.	110 William Street 9th FLR	New York	NY	10038	212-255-1122 212-645-1638
Huey Min Chuang	Business Outreach Center	125 Canal Street STE 302	New York	NY	10002	212-966-7328 212-966-7501
Ron Deutsch	SENSES	275 State Street	Albany	NY	12210-1210	518 463-5576 518 432-9073

NAME	ORGANIZATION	ADDRESS	CITY	STATE	ZIP CODE	TEL/FAX #
Joanne M. Oplustil	CAMBA	1720 Church Avenue	Brooklyn	NY	11226	718 287-2600 718 856-4647
A. Peck	Catskill Watershed Corporation	PO Box 569 Main Street	Margaret-ville	NY	12455-0569	914-586-1400 914-586-1401
Gerry Souzis	Chinatown Manpower Project	125 Canal Street Room 302	New York	NY	10002	212-966-7328 212-966-7501
Meg Barnette	Community Development Venture Capital Alliance	9 East 47th Street, 5th FLR	New York	NY	10017-1904	212-980-6790 212-980-6791
Nick Schatzki	Emek Group Inc.	88 Pine Street Floor 20	New York	NY	10005-1081	212-690-2024 212-690-2028
Maria Padilla Orasel	Empire State Development	633 Third Avenue 32nd Floor	New York	NY	10017	212-803-2410 212-803-2459
Karen Prudente	General Board of Global Ministries, United Methodist Church Women's Division	475 Riverside Drive #1503	New York	NY	10115	212-870-3739 212-870-3736
Josephine Infante	Hunts Point Economic Development Corporation	355 Food Center Drive C104	Bronx	NY	10474	718-842-1717 718-842-6592
Jennifer Thompson	Lower East Side Peoples Federal Credit Union	37 Avenue B	New York	NY	10001	
Anna Wadia	Ms. Foundation for Women	120 Wall Street, 33rd FLR	New York	NY	10005-3904	212-742-2300 212-742-1653
Clifford Rosenthal	National Federation of Community Development Credit Unions	120 Wall Street, 10th Floor	New York	NY	10005	212-809-1850 212-809-3274
Peter Sheridan	New York State Office of Mental Retardation and Development Disabilities	44 Holland Avenue	Albany	NY	12229	
Mary Ros	New York Association for New Americans, Inc.	17 Battery Place	New York	NY	10004	212-425-5051 212-425-7260
James Marshall	World Relief	201 Rt. 9W North	Congers	NY	10920	914 268-4135 914 268-2271
Jose Cruz	Worker Owner Resource Center	One Franklin Square, Exchange St.	Geneva	NY	14456-1801	315 789-5091 315 789-0261
Ruth B. Cowan	Pro Mujer	320 Central Park West #8G	New York	NY	10025	212 787-0181 121-787-0181
Thomas V. Seessel	SEEDCO	915 Broadway Suite 1703	New York	NY	10010-7106	212 473-0255 212 473-0357
Alvin Goode	NY Empire State Development Entrepreneur Assistance Program	87 South Broadway	Yonkers	NY	10701	914-963-3865 914-963-3865
Tanya Chauhan	Renaissance Economic Development Corporation	180 Eldridge Street	New York	NY	10002	212-979-8988 212-979-8811
Umar Mustafaa	Sector 4 Community Development Corporation	803 West Avenue	Rochester	NY	14611	716-328-5750 716-328-7351

NAME	ORGANIZATION	ADDRESS	CITY	STATE	ZIP CODE	TEL/FAX #
U. Alford	Springfield Baptist Church Rheedlen Centers	157 West 122nd Street	New York	NY	10027	212-932-1920 212-663-2590
Anne Janiak	Women's Enterprise Project Inc.	707 Westchester Ave., STE 213	White Plains	NY	10604	914-948-6444 914-948-6913
Maria Semidei Otero	Women's Venture Fund	45 John Street STE 1009	New York	NY	10038	212-732-7500 212-732-2296
Mary Hinton	Workshop in Business Opportunities	23 Gramercy Park South	New York	NY	10003	212-982-6925 212-982-6886
Joan a. Dallis	Rural Opportunities, Inc.	400 East Avenue Suite 401	Rochester	NY	14607	716-340-3385 716-340-3326
Debra McBride	Women's Business Resource Program of Southeast Ohio	20 E. Circle Dr. #155 Technology & Enterprise Building	Athens	OH	45701	740-593-1792 740-593-1795
Rahim Spence	Smart Money Community Services	1731 Vine Street	Cincinnati	OH	45010	513 241-7266 513 241-7436
Rosaline A. Brewster	Glenville Development Corp.	10640 St. Clair	Cleveland	OH	44108	216 851-8724 216 851-8941
Laurie Murphy	WECO	2700 E. 79th Street	Cleveland	OH	44104	216 881-9650 216 881-9704
Bob Cohen	ACDI VOCA	6161 Busch Blvd. Suite. 209	Columbus	OH	43229-2554	614 844-5820 614 844-5825
Mary Ann McClure	OWBRN	77 S. High Street 28th Floor	Columbus	OH	43215-6108	614 466-2682 614-466-0829
Evelyn C. France	Women's Development Center Inc.	1005 N. Abbe Road	Elyria	OH	44035-1613	440-324-3384
Michelle I. Spain	Western Reserve Minority C of C	20475 Farnsleigh Road Suite 105	Shaker Heights	OH	44122-3850	216 283-4700 216 283-5006
June Holley	Appalachian Center for Economic Networks	94 N. Columbus Road	Athens	OH	45701	740-593-5451 614-593-5451
Andrea Patterson	Columbus Countywide Development Corporation	941 Chatham Lane, Suite 300	Columbus	OH	43221-2416	614-645-6171 614-645-8588
Deborah North	Enterprise Works	88 E. Broad Street, Suite 1770	Columbus	OH	43215	614-460-6193 614-460-6110
Alicia Townsend	Greater Cincinnati Microenterprise Initiative Inc.	3011 Woodburn Avenue	Cincinnati	OH	45206	513-569-1240 513-961-2220
Inna Kinney	Jewish Family Services	1151 Collage Avenue	Columbus	OH	43209	614-231-1890 614-231-4978
Dinah Adkins	National Business Incubation Association	20 East Circle Drive Suite 190	Athens	OH	45701	740-593-4331 740-593-1996
Janice Robinson	Women's Organization for Mentoring Entrepreneurship and Networking	526 S. Main Street Suite 235	Akron	OH	44311-4403	330-379-9280 330-379-3454
Erin Randel	Ohio CDC Association	85 E. Gay Street Suite 403	Columbus	OH	43215-3118	614-461-6392 614-461-1011
Laura Lucas	Logan County Metropolitan Housing Authority	116 N. Everett	Bellefontaine	OH	43311	937-599-1845 937-592-7064

NAME	ORGANIZATION	ADDRESS	CITY	STATE	ZIP CODE	TEL/FAX #
Karen A. Patton	Enterprise Development Corp.	9030 Hocking Hills Drive	The Plains	OH	45780-1209	740-797-9646 740-797-9659
Sam Peled	Community Action Project of Tulsa County	717 S. Houston Ave., Suite 200	Tulsa	OK	74127-9005	918-835-2882 918-835-2883
Anna Knight	Cherokee Nation	PO Box 948	Tahlequah	OK	74464	918-456-0671 918-458-4295
Deborah Hart	OUR Federal Credit Union	715 Lincoln Street	Eugene	OR	97401	541-485-1188 541-485-3070
Karen Scriven	Mercy Corps International Refugee Immigrant Self Employment Program	3030 SW First Avenue	Portland	OR	97201	503-796-6800 503-796-6843
Rene Toman	Umpiqua Community Development Corporation	738 SE Kane Street	Roseburg	OR	97470	541-673-4909 541-673-5023
Mary O'Kief	Southern Oregon Women's Access to Credit Inc.	33 N. Central Suite 209	Medford	OR	97501	541-779-3992 541-779-5195
Julie Thomases	Community Action Development Corp. of Leigh Valley	605 Turner Street	Allentown	PA	18102	610 433-5703 610 433-2446
Joseph Fest	Rural Enterprise Development Corp	180 Chestnut Street	Bloomsburg	PA	17815-2027	570-784-7003 570-784-7030
Howard Good	Mennonite Economic Development Association	1821 Oregon Pike Suite 201	Lancaster	PA	17601	717 560-6546 717 560-6549
Jim Williams	ASSETS MONTCO	3 E Marshall Street	Norristown	PA	19401	610 275-3520 610 272-7802
Leslie Esdaile	Ben Franklin Technology Center	11 Penn Center 1835 Market Street Suite 1100	Philadelphia	PA	19103	215-972-6700 215-972-5588
Lynne Cutler	WORC	1930 Chestnut Street Suite 1600	Philadelphia	PA	19103	215 564-5500 215 564-0933
Sharon K. Williams	Minority Enterprise Corp. of Soutwestern PA	1801 Centre Avenue Suite 208	Pittsburgh	PA	15219-4305	412-434-5806 412-434-5881
Jill Mahon	Kutztown University EDGE Center	601 Penn Street	Reading	PA	19603-0253	610 375-4220 610 375-4229
Ronald J. Errett	Mercer County Community Action	296 A Street P.O. Box 667	Sharon	PA	16146-0667	412 342-6222 412 342-6295
Suse Greenstone	Creation Continues Educational Services	895 Red Rock Road	Gettysburg	PA	17325	717-337-3175 717-337-3175
Iola Carter	Lutheran Children and Family Service	45 Garrett Road	Upper Darby	PA	19082-2302	215-387-1700 215-387-7187
Fred Abrams	Pennsylvania Department of Community and Economic Development	Community Empowerment Office Room 357 Forum Building	Harrisburg	PA	17120	717-787-4140 717-234-4560
Linda Karl	Philadelphia Commercial Development Corporation	1315 Walnut Street Suite 600	Philadelphia	PA	19107-4706	215-790-2210 215-790-5016
Jeremiah White	Philadelphia Development Partnership	1334 Walnut Street, 7th Floor	Philadelphia	PA	19107	215-545-3100 215-546-8055

NAME	ORGANIZATION	ADDRESS	CITY	STATE	ZIP CODE	TEL/FAX #
Amanda Joseph	Shefa Fund	805 East Willow Grove Avenue	Wyndmoor	PA	19038	215-247-9704 215-247-1015
Rahim Islam	Universal Community Homes	800 South 15th Street	Philadelphia	PA	19146	215-732-6518 215-732-6519
Michael Mignogna	Southern Alleghenies Planning and Development Commission	541 58th Street	Altoona	PA	16602	814-949-6547 814-949-6505
Rick Beaton	Montgomery County Community Action Development Commission	113 E. Main Street	Norristown	PA	19401-4916	610-277-6367 610-277-7399
Malcom L. Morgan	Washington County Council on Economic Development	100 West Beau Street Suite 703	Washington	PA	15301	412 228-6816 412 250-6502
Beulah White	Five Rivers Community Development Corporation	PO Box 1279	Georgetown	SC	29442	843-527-4596 843-527-3878
Joanne Emerson	Interfaith Community Services of SC, Inc.	PO Box 11570	Columbia	SC	29211-1570	800-879-2219 803-799-1572
Robert Hull	NE South Dakota Community Action Project	414 Third Avenue E	Sisseton	SD	57262	605 698-7654 605 698-3038
Chanda Freeman	Area Relief Ministries	PO Box 7 301 N Hays Avenue	Jackson	TN	38301	901-423-9257 901-423-0284
Henry Garant	East Tennessee Community Design Center	1522 Highland Avenue	Knoxville	TN	37916	615-525-9945 615-693-8905
Tom Anderson	East Tennessee State University Community Partnership Center	603 Bert Street Suite 209	Johnson City	TN	37601	423-232-5750 423-232-5740
Benita Davis	EGT Inc. Working Smart	78 Layfayette Street Suite 8	Nashville	TN	37210	615-726-0181 615-726-0183
Michele Flynn	TN Network for Community Economic Development	P.O. Box 23353	Nashville	TN	37202	615-248-3130 615-256-9836
Cleo Johnson McLaughlin	Black United Fund of Texas	5407 Chenevert	Houston	TX	77004	713-524-5767 713-524-5769
Tony Johnson	The Promised Land Network	P.O. Box 1844	Hereford	TX	79045	806-364-4445 806-364-4005
Jeanette Peten	Business in Growth	1009 E. 11th Street Suite 216	Houston	TX	78702	512-494-8044 512-494-8043
Amos Brown	Corporation for Economic Development of Harris, Co	2223 West Loop Street #400	Houston	TX	77027-3588	713-840-8804 713-840-8806
Omar Ontiveros	El Puente Community Development Inc.	2000 Texas	EL Paso	TX	79901	915-533-7378 915-544-3730
Clarissa Chavez	FEMAP Foundation	415 E. Yandell Suite 120	El Paso	TX	79902	915-544-4151 915-496-8508
Gwen Moore	Plan Fund	729 North Bishop Avenue	Dallas	TX	75208	214-943-9007 214-948-4830

NAME	ORGANIZATION	ADDRESS	CITY	STATE	ZIP CODE	TEL/FAX #
Alma Smith	YWCA Women's Enterprise Program	405 N. St. Mary's #500	San Antonio	TX	78205	210-228-9922 210-228-9949
Elizabeth Rhodes	Texas A&M University Colonias Program	2002 Fremont Street	Laredo	TX	78043	956-728-0210 956-728-0219
Carol Coston	Partners for the Common Good 2000	2507 NW 36th Street	San Antonio	TX	78228	210-431-0616 210-431-0161
Kathy J. Ricci	Utha Microenterprise Loan Fund	3595 S. Main Street	Salt Lake City	UT	84115	801-269-8408 801-269-1063
Welthy H. Soni	BusinessStart	C/O People Inc. 1173 W. Main Street	Abingdom	VA	24210	540 619-2239 540 628-2931
Tsehaye Teferra	Ethiopian Community Development Council, Inc.	1038 S. Highland Street	Arlington	VA	22204	703 685-0510 703 685-0529
Carla Brown	Department of Minority Business Enterprise	200-202 N. 9th Street, 11th FLR	Richmond	VA	23219	804-692-0122 804-786-9736
Monica Appleby	New Enterprises Fund	930 Cambria Street	Christian-burg	VA	24073	540-382-2002 540-382-1935
Georgia Emory	Enterprise Development International, Inc.	10395 Democracy Lane Suite B	Fairfax	VA	22030	703 277-3360 703 277-3348
Jeff Jeffers	First Nations Development Institute	The Stores Building 11917 Main Street	Fredericks-burg	VA	22408-7326	540 371-5615 540 371-3505
Richard L. Stallings	Business Development Center	147 Mill Ridge Road	Lynchburg	VA	24502	804 582-6100 804 582-6106
Charles Skala	Franklin County Chamber of Commerce	261 Franklin Street PO Box 158	Rocky Mount	VA	24151	540-483-9542 540-483-0653
Bruce Asberry	Porstmouth Community Development Group	440 High Street Suite 204	Porstmouth	VA	23704	757-399-0925 7575-399-
Stephen Schley	Richmond Economic Development Corporation	530 E. Main Street #510	Richmond	VA	23219	804-780-3013 804-788-4310
Ellen Garren	Town of Pulaski Virginia Pulaski Venture Fund	PO Box 660	Pulaski	VA	24301	540-994-8636 540-994-8632
M. Hollifield	Virginia Department of Housing and Community Development	501 North Second Street	Richmond	VA	23219	804-371-7030 804-371-7093
Robert Manoil	Virginia Eastern Shore Economic Empowerment and Housing Corporation	PO Box 814	Nassawadox	VA	23413	757-442-4509 757-442-7530
Janet Dob	Virginia Economic Development Corporation	PO Box 1505 300 East Main Street	Charlottes-ville	VA	22902-1505	804-979-0114 804-979-1597
Mary R. Niebling	Central Vermont Community Act.	195 US Route 302-Berlin	Barre	VT	05641	802 479-1053 802 479-5353
Jim White	Champlain Calley Office of Economic Opp. Inc.	95 North Avenue	Burlington	VT	05401	802-860-1417 802-860-1387
Bridget H. Conroy	Vermont Department of Employment & Training	5 Green Mountain Drive	Montpelier	VT	05601	802 828-4000 802 828-4374

NAME	ORGANIZATION	ADDRESS	CITY	STATE	ZIP CODE	TEL/FAX #
Hope L. Campbell	Vermont Economic Development Authority	58 E. State Street	Montpelier	VT	05602	802 828-5467 802 828-5474
Reta Chaffe	Micro Business Development Program	91 Buck Drive	Westminster	VT	05158	802 722-4575 802 722-4509
Richard Sola	Eastern Washington University	705 W. 1st Avenue #223	Spokane	WA	99201-3909	509-623-4248 509-623-4230
Emily Duncan	Snohomish County Private Industry Council	728 134th Street SW #219	Everett	WA	98204	425-743-9669 425-742-1177
Judy Allen	Community Action Center	105 Main Street Suite 1	Pullman	WA	99163	509-334-9147 509-334-9105
Diahann Howard	Tri-Cities Enterprise Association	2000 Logston Blvd.	Richland	WA	99352	509-375-3268 509-375-4838
Shaw Canale	Cascadia Revolving Fund	119 1st Avenue Suite 100	Seattle	WA	98104-2533	206-447-9226 206-682-4804
Harriet Stephenson	Seattle University Albers School of Business and Economics	900 Broadway	Seattle	WA	98122-4340	206-296-5730 206-296-5795
Peter W. Rose	Washington Cash	410 Boston Street	Seattle	WA	98109-2127	206-729-8589 206 729-8589
Teresa Lemmons	Tacoma Metropolitan Development Council	202 North Tacoma Ave. #D	Tacoma	WA	98403	253-591-7026 253-572-5583
Sally Schrader	Indianhead Community Action Agency	PO Box 40	Ladysmith	WI	54848	715-532-5594 715-532-7808
Daniel Magnuson	Ways to Work	11700 W. Lake Park Drive	Milwaukee	WI	53224	414-359-1040 414-359-1074
Karla Miller	West Central Wisconsin Comm. Action Agency	119 West 6th Avenue	Menomonie	WI	54751	715-235-8525 715-235-8695
Mary Streff	Wisconsin Coulee Region Community Action Program	201 Melby Street	Westby	WI	54667	608-634-7364 608-634-3134
Wendy Werkmeister	Wisconsin Women's Business Initiative Corp.	2821 N. 4th Street	Milwaukee	WI	53212	414-263-5450 414-263-5456
Marjorie Kozich	Wisconsin Housing and Economic Development Authority	PO Box 1728	Madison	WI	53701-1728	608-266-7643 608-267-1099
Renee Walz	Western Dairyland EOC	23122 Whithall Road PO Box 45	Independence	WI	54747-0045	715-985-2391 715-985-3239
Pam Curry	Center for Economic Options Inc.	601 Delaware Avenue	Charleston	WV	25320	304-345-1298 304-342-0641
Kevin Brady	Wirt County Development Authority	823 Schoolview Street Box 775	Elizabeth	WV	26143	304-275-4759 304-275-4761
Diane L. Browning	Appalachian By Design	208 S. Court Street	Lewisburg	WV	24901	304 647-3455 304 647-3466
Carlos Gasca	Mennonite Central Commission Employment Development	162936 Radcliffe Drive SE	Calgary	Alberta	T2A6M8	403-272-9323 403-235-4646
Roland Vanderburg	MCC Employment Development	2936 Radcliffe Drive SE #16	Calgary	Alberta	T2A6M8	403 272-9323 403 235-4646

NAME	ORGANIZATION	ADDRESS	CITY	STATE	ZIP CODE	TEL/FAX #
Ingrid Fischer	VanCity Credit Union	183 Terminal Avenue	Vancover	British Columbia	V6B1A1	604 708-7860 604 688-7052
Carol Rock	Women and Rural Economic Development	379 Huron Street	Stratford	Ontario	N0K1P0	519-273-5017 519-273-4826
Nanci Lee	Calmeadow	365 Bay Street Suite 600	Toronto	Ontario	M5H2V1	416-362-9670 416-362-0769
Peter Nares	Self employment Development Initiatives (SEDI)	1110 Finch Avenue West Suite 406	Toronto	Ontario	M3J2T2	416-665-2828 416-504-8738
Erika Watson	Women's Employment, Enterprise & Training Unit	Suite 2, Floor 2, Sackville Place 44-48 Magdalen Street	Norwich, Norfolk	England	NR31JU	44-1603-767367 44-1603-666693

MICROLENDERS/SERVICE PROVIDER CONTACTS

NAME	TELEPHONE NUMBER ADDRESS	NOTES

ACCOUNTANTS FOR THE PUBLIC INTEREST

The following list of accountants provide services at a reduce fee. If there is not an office near you, call one of the affiliates and asked to be referred to an accountant who does volunteer consulting in your city.

STATE	OFFICE	ADDRESS	TELEPHONE FAX #	CONTACT NAME
CA	Clearinghouse for Volunteer Accounting Services	27863 Lassen Street Castaic, CA 91384	805 295-8912 805 295-8333	Ms. Lamson
CT	Community Accounting Aid and Services Inc.	1800 Asylum Avenue 4th Floor West Hartford, CT 06117	806 570-9113 860 570-9107	Nancy K.DeAngelis
FL	Florida Association of Nonprofit Organizations	7480 Fairway Drive Suite 206 Miami Lakes, FL 33014	305 557-1764 305 821-5228	Marina Pavlov President
GA	Nonprofit Resource Center	The Hurt Building Suite 220 Atlanta, GA 30303	404 688-4845 404 521-0487	Pam Sugerman
IL	CPA for the Public Interest	222 S. Riverside Plaza 16th Floor Chicago, IL 60606	312 993-0407 ext. 243 312 993-9432	Susan Salisbury-Richards Executive Director
IN	Quality For Indiana Taxpayers, Inc.	429 N. Pennsylvania Street #101 Indianapolis, IN 46204	317 974-0736 317 226-5724	Stuart Sobel
MD	Maryland Association of Nonprofit Organizations	190 W. Ostend Street Suite 201 Baltimore, MD 21230	410 727-6367- 800 273-6367 410 727-1914	Nancy Hall Director of Finance
MA	Community Tax Aid, Inc.	c/o Arthur Andersen, LLP 225 Franklin Street Boston, MA 02110	617 330-4721 617 439-9731	Brian P. MacArthur
MI	Accounting Aid Society	One Kennedy Square 719 Griswold Suite 2026 Detroit, MI 48226	313 961-1840 313 961-6257	Cynthia Tanner President

STATE	OFFICE	ADDRESS	TELEPHONE FAX #	CONTACT NAME
MN	Minnesota Accounting Aid Society	1806 South Riverside Ave Minneapolis, MN 55454	612 288-9476 612 288-9597	Jill Schwimmer Executive Director
MS	Mississippi Center for Nonprofits, Inc.	612 North State Street Suite B Jackson ,MS 39202	601 968-0061 601 352-8820	Nathan Woodliff Stanely
NJ	Accountants for the Public Interest	214 Route 18 North East Brunswick, NJ 08816	732 249-7565 732 249-8158	
NY	Community Tax Aid, Inc. NY Support Center for Non Profit Mgmt	176 E. 85th Street 4 C New York, NY 10025		
PA	Community Accountants	1420 Walnut Street Suite 411 Philadelphia, PA 19102	215 893-9333 215 893-9339	Maurine Dooley Executive Director
PA	Western Pennsylvania Community Accountants, Inc.	425 6th Avenue #1890 Pittsburgh, PA 15219	412 434-1611 412 434-8234	Harmony Greene
RI	Support Center of Rhode Island Volunteer Accounting Program	10 Davol Square 3rd Floor Providence, RI 02903-4752	401 861-1920 or 401 861-1921 401 273-0540	Neil Sharp
VA	Virginia Society of CPAs Public Service Volunteer Program	P.O. Box 4620 Richmond, VA 23058-4620	804 270-5344 804 273-1741	Julie Chamberlain Public Relations Director
WI	Wisconsin Institute of CPAs Public Interest Committee	235 N. Executive Drive Suite 200 Brookfield, WI 53008-1010	414 785-0445 or 800 772-6939 414 785-0838	Mary Williamson

ARTS AGENCIES
STATE, REGIONAL AND JURISDICTIONAL

The following list includes state and jurisdictional arts agencies and regional arts organizations that work with the Arts Endowment and utilizes funds mandated by Congress as well as funds from state governments and other sources.

NAME	ADDRESS	TELEPHONE NUMBER	INTERNET ADDRESS
National Assembly of State Arts Agencies	1029 Vermont Avenue, NW 2nd Floor Washington, DC 20005	202 347-6352	nasaa@nasaa-arts.org
Americans for the Arts	1000 Vermont Avenue, NW 12th Floor Washington, DC 20005	202 371-2830	nalaamem@artswire.org
Arts Midwest	Hennepin Center for the Arts 528 Hennepin Avenue, Suite 310 Minneapolis, MN 55403	612 341-0755 TT/Voice: 612/341-0901	webcom@artsmidwest.org
Consortium for Pacific Arts & Cultures	2141C Atherton Road Honolulu, HI 96822	808 946-7381	
Mid-America Arts Alliance	912 Baltimore Avenue, Suite 700 Kansas City, MO 64105	816 421-1388	maaa.org
Mid Atlantic Arts Foundation	22 Light Street, #330 Baltimore, MD 21202	410 539-6656 TT: 410 539-4241	maaf@midarts.usa.com
New England Foundation for the Arts	330 Congress Street, 6th Fl. Boston, MA 02210-1216	617 951-0010	info@nefa.org
Southern Arts Federation	1401 Peachtree Street, Suite 460 Atlanta, GA 30309	404 874-7244 TT: 404 876-6240	southarts.org
Western States Arts Federation	1543 Champa St., Suite 220 Denver, CO 80202	303-629-1166	staff@westaf.org
Alabama State Council on the Arts	One Dexter Avenue Montgomery, AL 36130	334 242-4076 TT/Relay: 800-548-2546	arts.state.al.us
Alaska State Council on the Arts	411 West 4th Avenue, Suite 1E Anchorage, AK 99501-2343	907/269-6610	asca@alaska.net
American Samoa Council on Arts, Culture & Humanities	P.O. Box 1540 Pago Pago, American Samoa 96799	011-684-633-4347	
Arizona Commission on the Arts	417 West Roosevelt Phoenix, AZ 85003	602 255-5882	general@ArizonaArts.org

NAME	ADDRESS	TELEPHONE NUMBER	INTERNET ADDRESS
Arkansas Arts Council	1500 Tower Building 323 Center Street Little Rock, AR 72201	501 324-9766	info@dah.state.ar.us
California Arts Council	1300 I Street, #930 Sacramento, CA 95814	916 322-6555 TT: 916 322-6569	cac@cwo.com
Colorado Council on the Arts	750 Pennsylvania Street Denver, CO 80203-3699	303 894-2617 TT: 303 894-2664	coloarts@artswire.org
Connecticut Commission on the Arts	Gold Building 755 Main Street Hartford, CT 06103	860 566-4770	cslnet.ctstateu.edu/cca/
Delaware Division of the Arts	State Office Building 820 North French Street Wilmington, DE 19801	302 577-3540 TT/Relay: 800-232-5460	delarts@artswire.org
District of Columbia Commission on the Arts & Humanities	410 8th Street, NW Washington, DC 20004	202 724-5613 TT: 202 727-3148	carrien@tmn.com
Division of Cultural Affairs	Florida Department of State The Capitol Tallahassee, FL 32399-0250	904 487-2980 TT: 904 488-5779	dos.state.fl.us/dca/
Georgia Council for the Arts	530 Means Street, NW Suite 115 Atlanta, GA 30318-5730	404 651-7920	gca@gwins.campus.mci.net
Guam Council on the Arts & Humanities	Office of the Governor P.O. Box 2950 Agana, GU 96910	011-671-647-2242	arts@ns.gov.nu
State Foundation on Culture & the Arts	44 Merchant Street Honolulu, HI 96813	808 586-0300 TTD: 808 586-0740	sfca@sfca.state.hi.us
Idaho Commission on the Arts	P.O. Box 83720 Boise, ID 83720-0008	208 334-2119	idarts@artswire.org
Illinois Arts Council	State of Illinois Center 100 West Randolph Suite 10-500 Chicago, IL 60601	312 814-6750 TT: 312 814-4831	ilarts@artswire.org
Indiana Arts Commission	402 West Washington Street, Room 072 Indianapolis, IN 46204-2741	317 232-1268 TT: 317 233-3001	inarts@aol.com
Iowa Arts Council	600 East Locust State Capitol Complex Des Moines, IA 50319	515 281-4451	jbailey@max.state.ia.us

NAME	ADDRESS	TELEPHONE NUMBER	INTERNET ADDRESS
Kentucky Arts Council	31 Fountain Place Frankfort, KY 40601	502 564-3757	State.ky.us/a gencies/arts/k achome.html
Division of the Arts	Louisiana Department of Culture, Recreation, & Tourism 1051 North 3rd Street P.O. Box 44247 Baton Rouge, LA 70804	504 342-8180	arts@crt.state .la.us
Maine Arts Commission	55 Capitol Street State House Station 25 Augusta, ME 04333	207 287-2724 TT: 207 287-5613	mainearts. com
Maryland State Arts Council	601 North Howard Street 1st Floor Baltimore, MD 21201	410 767-6555	msac@digex. net
Massachusetts Cultural Council	120 Boylston Street 2nd Floor Boston, MA 02116-4600	617 727-3668 TT: 617 338-9153	massculture council.org
Michigan Council for Arts and Cultural Affairs	525 West Ottawa Street P.O. Box 30705 Lansing, MI 48909-8205	517 241-4011	commerce. state.mi. us/arts
Minnesota State Arts Board	Park Square Court 400 Sibley Street, Suite 200 St. Paul, MN 55101-1949	612 215-1600 800 8MN-ARTS TT/Relay: 612/297-5353	msab@tc. umn.edu
Mississippi Arts Commission	239 North Lamar Street Second Floor Jackson, MS 39201	601 359-6030	arts.state.ms. us
Missouri State Council on the Arts	Wainwright Office Complex 111 North Seventh Street Suite 105 St. Louis, MO 63101	314 340-6845	mac@state. mt.us
Montana Arts Council	316 North Park Avenue Room 252 Helena, MT 59620	406 444-6430 TT/Relay: 800-833-8503	mac@state. mt.us
Nebraska Arts Council	The Joslyn Castle Carriage House 3838 Davenport Street Omaha, NE 68131-2329	402 595-2122 TT/Voice: 402 595-2122	nacart@ synergy.net
Nevada Arts Council	Capitol Complex 602 North Curry Street Carson City, NV 89710	702 687-6680	

NAME	ADDRESS	TELEPHONE NUMBER	INTERNET ADDRESS
New Jersey State Council on the Arts	20 West State Street, # 306 Trenton, NJ 08625-0306	609 292-6130 TT: 609 633-1186	njartscouncil. org
New Mexico Arts Division	228 East Palace Avenue Santa Fe, NM 87501	505 827-6490 TT: 505 827-6925	artadmin@ oca.state.nm. us
New York State Council on the Arts	915 Broadway New York, NY 10010	212 387-7000 TT: 212 387-7049	nysca@ artswire.org
North Carolina Arts Council	Department of Cultural Resources Raleigh, NC 27601-2807	919 733-2821	ncarts.org
North Dakota Council on the Arts	418 East Broadway Ave. Suite 70 Bismarck, ND 58501-4086	701 328-3954	thompson@ pioneer.state. nd.us
Commonwealth Council for Arts & Culture	P.O. Box 553, CHRB CNMI Convention Center Commonwealth of the Northern Mariana Islands Saipan, MP 96950	9-011-670-322-9982	
Ohio Arts Council	727 East Main Street Columbus, OH 43205	614 466-2613 TT: 614 466-4541	bfisher@mail .oac.ohio.gov wlawson@ mail.oac.ohio .gov
Oklahoma Arts Council	P.O. Box 52001-2001 Oklahoma City, OK 73152-2001	405 521-2931	okarts@tmn. com
Oregon Arts Commission	775 Summer Street, NE Salem, OR 97310	503 986-0082 TT: 503 378-3772	oregon.artsco mm@State. OR.US
Commonwealth of Pennsylvania Council on the Arts	Finance Building, Room 216A Harrisburg, PA 17120	717 787-6883 TT/Relay: 800 654-5984	artsnet.heinz. cmu.edu/pca/
Institute of Puerto Rican Culture	Apartado Postal 4184 San Juan, PR 00902-4184	809 723-2115	
Rhode Island State Council on the Arts	95 Cedar Street, Suite 103 Providence, RI 02903	401 277-3880 TT: 401 277-3880	info@risca. state.ri.us
South Carolina Arts Commission	1800 Gervais Street Columbia, SC 29201	803 734-8696	kenmay@ scsn.net
South Dakota Arts Council	Office of Arts 800 Governors Drive Pierre, SD 57501-2294	605 773-3131 TT/Relay: 800-622-1770	sdac@stlib. state.sd.us

NAME	ADDRESS	TELEPHONE NUMBER	INTERNET ADDRESS
Texas Commission on the Arts	P.O. Box 13406 Austin, TX 78711-3406	512 463-5535 TTY: 512 475-3327	front.desk@ arts.state.tx. us
Utah Arts Council	617 East South Temple St. Salt Lake City, UT 84102	801 533-5895	dadamson@ email.st.ut.us
Vermont Arts Council	136 State Street Montpelier, VT 05633-6001	802 828-3291 TT/Relay: 800 253-0191	info@arts. vca.state.vt. us
<u>Virginia Commission for the Arts</u>	223 Governor Street Richmond, VA 23219	804 225-3132 TT: 804 225-3132	vacomm@art swire.org
Virgin Islands Council on the Arts	41-42 Norre Gade, 2nd Floor P.O. Box 103 St. Thomas, VI 00802	340 774-5984	
Washington State Arts Commission	234 East 8th Avenue P.O. Box 42675 Olympia, WA 98504-2675	360 753-3860 TT/Relay: 206 554-7400 or 800-833-6388	wsac@ artswire.org
Arts & Humanities Section	West Virginia Division of Culture & History 1900 Kanawha Blvd. East Capitol Complex Charleston, WV 25305-0300	304 558-0220 TT: 304 348-0220	wvlc.wvnet. edu/culture/ arts
West Virginia Division of Culture & History	1900 Kanawha Blvd. East Capitol Complex Charleston, WV 25305-0300	304 558-0220 TT: 304 348-0220	wvlc.wvnet.e du/culture/ arts.
Wisconsin Arts Board	101 East Wilson Street 1st Floor Madison, WI 53702	608 266-0190 TT: 608 267-9629	arts.state.wi. us
Wyoming Arts Council	2320 Capitol Avenue Cheyenne, WY 82002	307 777-7742 TT: 307 777-5964	wyoarts@arts wire.org

ART AGENCIES TO CONTACT

NAME	ADDRESS	TELEPHONE NUMBER	INTERNET ADDRESS

SMALL BUSINESS DEVELOPMENT CENTERS (SBDC)

SBDC's coordinate federal, state, local, university and private resources in counseling and training small business owners. A wide range of services is available, including management and technical assistance as well as training and advice on marketing, finances, production and organization. The following numbers are for the lead SBDC in each state.

STATE	LEAD SBDC	TELEPHONE NUMBER
ALABAMA	University of Alabama at Birmingham	(205) 934-7260
ALASKA	University of Alaska at Anchorage	(907) 274-7232
ARIZONA	Arizona SBDC Network	(602) 731-8720
ARKANSAS	University of Arkansas at Little Rock	(501) 324-9043
CALIFORNIA	California Trade & Commerce Agency	(916) 325-5068
COLORADO	Office of Business Development	(303) 892-3809
CONNECTICUT	University of Connecticut	(860) 486-4135
DELAWARE	University of Delaware	(302) 831-1555
DISTRICT OF COLUMBIA	Howard University – Metropolitan Washington SBDC	(202) 806-1550
FLORIDA	University of West Florida	(904) 444-2060
GEORGIA	University of Georgia	(706) 542-6762
GUAM	University of Guam	671-735-2556
HAWAII	University of Hawaii at Hilo	(808) 933-3515
IDAHO	Boise State University	(208) 385-1640
ILLINOIS	Department of Commerce & Community Affairs	(217) 524-5856
INDIANA	Indiana Small Business Development Center	(317) 264-6871
IOWA	Iowa State University	(515) 292-6351
KANSAS	Wichita State University	(316) 689-3193
KENTUCKY	University of Kentucky	(606) 257-7668
LOUISIANA	Northeast Louisiana University	(318) 342-5506
MAINE	University of Southern Maine	(207) 780-4420

STATE	LEAD SBDC	TELEPHONE NUMBER
MARYLAND	Department of Economic & Employment Development	(410) 767-6552
MASSACHUSETTS	University of Massachusetts	(413) 545-6301
MICHIGAN	Wayne State University	(313) 964-1798
MINNESOTA	Department of Trade & Economic Development	(612) 297-5770
MISSISSIPPI	University of Mississippi	(601) 232-5001
MISSOURI	University of Missouri	(573) 882-0344
MONTANA	Montana Department of Commerce	(406) 444-4780
NEBRASKA	University of Nebraska at Omaha	(402) 554-2521
NEVADA	University of Nevada at Reno	(702) 784-1717
NEW HAMPSHIRE	University of New Hampshire	(603) 862-2200
NEW JERSEY	Rutgers University	(201) 648-5950
NEW MEXICO	Santa Fe Community College	(505) 438-1362
NEW YORK	State University of New York	(518) 443-5398
NORTH CAROLINA	University of North Carolina	(919) 571-4154
NORTH DAKOTA	University of North Dakota	(701) 777-3700
OHIO	Ohio Department of Development	(614) 466-2711
OKLAHOMA	Southeastern State University	(405) 924-0277
OREGON	Lane Community College	(503) 725-2250
PENNSYLVANIA	University of Pennsylvania	(215) 898-1219
PUERTO RICO	University of Puerto Rico at Mayaguez	(809) 834-3590
RHODE ISLAND	Bryant College SBDC	(401) 232-6111
SOUTH CAROLINA	University of South Carolina	(803) 777-4907
SOUTH DAKOTA	University of South Dakota	(605) 677-5498
TENNESSEE	University of Memphis	(901) 678-2500
TEXAS	Houston Small Business Development Center	(713) 752-8400

STATE	LEAD SBDC	TELEPHONE NUMBER
UTAH	University of Utah	(801) 255-5991
VERMONT	Vermont Technical College	(802) 728-9101
VIRGIN ISLANDS	University of the Virgin Islands	(809) 776-3206
VIRGINIA	Commonwealth of Virginia Department of Economic Development	(804) 371-8253
WASHINGTON	Washington State University	(509) 335-1576
WEST VIRGINIA	West Virginia Development Office	(304) 558-2960
WISCONSIN	University of Wisconsin	(608) 263-7794
WYOMING	University of Wyoming	(307) 766-3505

The SBA's Office of Advocacy publishes a book called *The States and Small Business: A Directory of Programs and Activities,* which gives more details on many of the programs and services. It is available from the Government Printing Office by call (202) 512-1800. The GPO stock number is 045-000-00266-7.

SMALL BUSINESS DEVELOPMENT CENTERS TO CALL

NAME	TELEPHONE NUMBER WEBSITE	NOTES

THE INTERNET REPRESENTS BIG ADVANTAGE FOR SMALL BUSINESS OWNERS AND SELF EMPLOYED ARTISTS

Virtual Internet competition is redefining the face of global commerce. Before you launch your business on the Internet, do your homework. Use it to research your competition. Immerse yourself in the Internet culture. Georgia Institute of Technology's Graphic, Visualization, and Usability Center, at the URL address http: www.cc.gatech.edu/gvu/user_surveys, provides a good overview of the typical Internet participant as well as a link http: www.cc.gatech.edu/gvu/user_surveys/others, to other sources on Internet statistics and demographics available on the Web. Do not rely on just one source or person to give you information. The more you learn about this powerful tool, the better equipped you'll be to develop a marketing plan that includes an on-line strategy. The following list contains Internet sites such as search engines, artist information, helpful business tools, "driving" directions etc.

SITE NAME	DESCRIPTION	INTERNET ADDRESS
ARTISTS NOW EXHIBITING WORK (A.N.E.W.)	Non-profit foundation for the arts providing financial and other assistance to professional artists from all disciplines	http://www.anew.org/
ASK JEEVES	I dare you to ask him any question that he can't answer!	http://www.ask.com/index.asp?origin=847 (also found on What Is)
AMERICAN COMPUTER RESOURCES, INC.	A guide to online resources specific to international trade. Alphabetical listing of International Country/City and US Area codes, zip codes etc.	http://www.the-acr.com/
ANGEL CAPITAL ELECTRONIC NETWORK (ACENET)	Financing resource	www.angelalliancenetwork.com or www.conan.net/promote/angelinvestor
BARTER ADVANTAGE	Trading your company's service or product for another service or product.	www.barteradv.com
BUSINESS FUNDING DIRECTORY	Provides potential sources of funding based on type of financing & your business characteristics.	http://www.businessfinance.com

SITE NAME	DESCRIPTION	INTERNET ADDRESS
COPYRIGHT OFFICE	Information about copyrights & downloadable applications.	http://www.cweb.loc.gov/ copyright
CORPORATE FINANCE NETWORK	Provides links to five lenders actively seeking to lend to small businesses.	http://www.corpfinet.com/ Small_Bus.html
CREATIVE CAPITAL	A revolving fund designed to support artists who pursue innovative approaches to content.	www.creative-capital.org
CREDIT FYI	A quick way to examine the credit history of a firm before you do business with them.	http://www.creditfyi.com
CURRENCY CALCULATOR	Converts currency on line.	http://www.x-rates.com/calculator.html
DAILY EXCHANGE RATE	Displays exchange rate for over 65 countries	http://pacific.commerce.ubc .ca/xr/
DIRECTORY	Email addresses, etc.	http://www.bigfoot.com
DOGPILE	Search Engine that uses multi search engines to look for information you've requested	http://www.dogpile.com
ENTREPRENET	Free articles about raising money & evaluating business transactions.	http://www.enterprise.org/ enet/index.html
EXCITE MAPS	US driving directions, maps plus lots more	http://www.city.net/maps/
ESPECTRO FOR ARTISTS	Put your portfolio online	http://www.espectro.com
FREE STUFF CENTER	Lots of free stuff, resources, etc.	http://www.biginfo.net/
GLOBAL ACCESS TO TRADE & TECHNOLOGY	Links to organizations & businesses relating to international commerce.	http://www.gatts.com
HARMONIZED SYSTEM CODE LOOKUP	Exporters/importers can look up HS code for any product or service.	http://www.xport.net/plv/sp . html
HOTBOT	Search Engine containing over 54 million Web pages	http://www.hotbot.com
IBEX YELLOW PAGES	Lists exporting companies by subject.	http://www.cba.uh.edu/ ylowpages

SITE NAME	DESCRIPTION	INTERNET ADDRESS
IDEA CAFÉ	Serving up practical business information in an entertaining manner. Get tips on raising capital and other start-up-related challenges.	http://www.ideacafe.com
INDUSTRY TRADE SHOWS & CONVENTIONS	Information about upcoming industry trade shows worldwide.	http://www.expoguide.com
INFOMARKET	Free & fee information available on many topics.	http://www.infomkt.ibm.com
MARKETING & ADVERTISING LINKS	Links to nonprofit & commercial sites about advertising & marketing.	http://www.bizmarketing.com/sites.html
NATIONAL ASSOCIATIONS OF TRADE EXCHANGES	An organization for trade exchange owners from across the country and around the world.	http://www.nate.org
NATIONAL ENDOWMENT FOR THE ARTS	Arts news, grants info and publications.	http://www.nea.endow.gov
NATIONAL FOUNDATION OF WOMEN BUSINESS OWNERS	Offers reports, news and trends affecting women, etc.	http://www.nfwbo.org
NATIONAL BUSINESSS INCUBATION ASSOCIATION	Provides protective environment for your business during the start-up stage.	www.nbia.org
NATIONAL NETWORK FOR ARTIST PLACEMENT (NNAP)	Listings of entry/intern/fellowship opportunities for Theatre Production, Music, Dance Film or Arts Management	http://members.aol.com/nnapnow/
PATENT & TRADMARK OFFICE	General information about patents & trademarks.	http://www.uspto.gov
PORT IMPORT EXPORT REPORTING SERVICE	Statistics about international shipments of goods.	http://www.piers.com
PRSA	Provides a gateway to organizations, individuals, products and services that are relevant to the responsibilities of a public relations professional	www.prsa.org

SITE NAME	DESCRIPTION	INTERNET ADDRESS
RESEARCH-IT	Dictionaries, thesaurus, language translators etc.	http://www.Tools.com/ research-it/research-it.html
SMALL BUSINESS CREDIT PROCESs	Describes the loan process for small businesses.	http://www.ny.frb.org/piho me/addpub/credit.html
SMALL BUSINESS RESOURCE CENTER	Useful reports on financing, writing business plan, etc.	http://www.webcom.com/ seaquest/srbc/welcome. html
SMALL BUSINESS TOOLKIT	Tools for small business planning & management.	http://www.toolkit.cch. com
SMALLBIZNET	Users can search a database of articles & books about all aspects of starting & running a small business.	http://www.lowe.org/smbiz net
WEBCINEMA	A nonprofit dedicated to the independent filmmaker using internet new medial technologies to finance, create, produce, distribute and market independent film.	http://webcinema.org/home. html
WELCOME TO THE INTERNET	Internet news, stock, technology, etc.	http://www.internet.com/
WHAT IS ?	Definition/topic containing the word or term you enter.	http://www.whatis.com
WOMEN NCORPORATED	Information on access to capital, credit, business discounts and products, and financial services.	http://www.womeninc. com/

VOLUNTEER LAWYERS FOR THE ARTS

Volunteer Lawyers for the Arts provide legal services to artists and arts groups. Some offices offer comprehensive services and others provided very limited service. For more specific information, contact the nearest office or contact Volunteer Lawyers for the Arts in New York, 513 319-5910, to request a Volunteer Lawyer for the Arts National Directory.

STATE	AGENCY	CITY	TEL. NO.
CA	California Lawyers for the Arts	San Francisco	415-775-7500
CA	California Lawyers for the Arts	Los Angeles	310-395-8893
Canada	Canadian Artists' Representation	Ontario	416-340-7791
Canada	Artist's Legal Advice Service Team	Toronto	416-360-0775
Canada	Artist's Legal Advice Service Team	Ottawa	613-567-5690
CO	Colorado Lawyers for the Arts	Denver	303-755-7994
CT	Connecticut Volunteer Lawyers for the Arts	Hartford	860-566-4770
DC	District of Columbia Lawyers for the Arts		505-459-0559
DC	Washington Area Lawyers for the Arts		505-393-5856
FL	Volunteer Lawyers for the Arts Florida	Fort Lauderdale	954-465-9191
GA	Georgia Volunteer Lawyers for the Arts	Atlanta	404-555-6046
IL	Lawyers for the Creative Arts	Chicago	315-944-5787
KS	Kansas Register of Volunteers for the Arts	Lindsborg	913-557-5351
LA	Louisiana Volunteer Lawyers for the Arts	New Orleans	504-553-1465
ME	Maine Volunteer Lawyers and Accountants for the Arts	Yarmouth	507-846-0640
MD	Maryland Lawyers for the Arts	Baltimore	410-755-1633

STATE	AGENCY	CITY	TEL. NO.
MA	Volunteer Lawyers for the Arts of Massachusetts	Boston	617-553-1764
MN	Resources and Counseling for the Arts	St. Paul	615-595-3506
MO	St. Louis Volunteer Lawyers and Accountants for the Arts	St. Louis	314-655-5410
MT	Montana Volunteer Lawyers for the Arts	Missoula	406-751-1835
NH	Lawyers for the Arts New Hampshire	Concord	603-554-8300
NY	Volunteer Lawyers for the Arts New York	New York	515-319-5787
NY	Art Law Line	New York	515-319-5910
OH	Volunteer Lawyers and Accountants for the Arts	Cleveland	516-696-3555
OH	Toledo Volunteer Lawyers for the Arts		419-555-3344
OR	Oregon Lawyers for the Arts	Portland	503-595-5787
PA	Volunteer Lawyers for the Arts	Philadelphia	515-545-3385
RI	Ocean State Lawyers for the Arts	Sauderstown	401-789-5686
SD	South Dakota Arts Council	Sioux Falls	605-339-6646
TX	Artists' Legal and Accounting Assistance	Austin	515-338-4458
TX	Texas Accountants and Lawyers for the Arts	Dallas	514-851-5555
		Houston	713-556-4876
UT	Utah Lawyers for the Arts	Salt Lake City	801-485-5373

WOMEN'S BUSINESS CENTERS

The Women's Business Centers were originally established by the SBA to assist and support women business owners with technical assistance. Operating in over sixty locations around the country, the Association of Women's Business Centers now provide a vast array of services ranging from entrepreneurial training to advocacy and financing. For information about the services the Women's Business Center in your state or city provides, please consult the following list.

ORGANIZATION NAME	ADDRESS	CITY	STATE	ZIP CODE	TEL/FAX#
Women's Business Assistance Center (WBAC)	P.O. Box 6021	Mobile	AL	36660	334 660-2725 334 660-8854
National Center for American Indian Enterprise Development (Arizona, Washington & California)	953 East Juanita Avenue	Mesa	AZ	85204	602 545-1298 602 491-1332
Woman's Economic Development Corp. (WEDC)	235 E. Broadway Suite 506	Long Beach	CA	90803	562 983-3747 562 983-3750
Woman's Economic Development Corp. (WEDC)	23301 Campus Drive Suite 20	Irvine	CA	92715	949 474-2933 949 474-7416
National Center for American Indian Enterprise Development, NW Region	9650 Flair Drive Suite 303	El Monte	CA	91731	818 442-3701 818 442-7115
WEST Company	340 N. Main St.	Fort Bragg	CA	95437	707 964-7571 707 981-1340
West Company (Parent Organization to WEST Co. Fort Bragg, CA)	367 North State Street Suite 208	Ukiah	CA	95482	707 468-3553 707 462-3555
WISE Oakland	519 17th Street Suite 520	Oakland	CA	94612	510 208-9473 510 208-9471
Women Business Owners Corporation	18 Encanto Drive	Palos Verdes	CA	90274-4215	310 530-7500 310 530-1483
Women's Initiative for Self-Employment (WISE) Parent Organization for WISE in Oakland	450 Mission Street Suite 402	San Francisco	CA	94102	415 247-9473 415 247-9471

ORGANIZATION NAME	ADDRESS	CITY	STATE	ZIP CODE	TEL/FAX#
Mi Casa Business Center for Women (BCW)	571 Galapago St.	Denver	CO	90204	303 573-1302 303 595-0422
American Woman's Economic Development Corp. (AWED)	2001 W. Main St. Suite 140	Stamford	CT	06902	203 326-7914
American Woman's Economic Development Corp. (Parent Organization to AWED)	1250 24th St. NW Room 120	Washington	DC	20037	202 857-0991 202 223-2775
National Council of Negro Women	633 Pennsylvania Ave. NW	Washington	DC`	20004	202 939-8104 202 939-8763
Women's Business Development Center (WBDC)	Florida International University OET-3	Miami	FL	33199	305 348-3951 305 348-2931
Coalition of 100 Black Women (Women's Economic Development Agency –WEDA)	The Chandler Building 127 Peachtree St. NE Suite 700	Atlanta	GA	30303	404 659-4008 404 659-3001
Women's Business Development Center (Parent for WBDC FL)	8 South Michigan Ave. Suite 400	Chicago	IL	60603	312 853-3477 312 853-0145
Women Entrepreneurs for Economic Development, Inc. (WEED)	210 O'Keefe Suite 300	New Orleans	LA	70112	504 524-5622 504 522-0096
Women Entrepreneurs for Economic Development, Inc. (WEED)	2245 Peters Rd.	Harvey	LA	70050	504 365-3866 504 365-3890
Center for Women and Enterprise, Inc.	45 Broomfield St. 6th Floor	Boston	MA	02106	617 423-3001 617 423-2444
Coastal Enterprises Inc.	P.O. Box 268	Wiscasset	ME	04578	207 882-7552 207 882-7308
Ann Arbor Community Development Corporation	2008 Hogback Road Suite 2A	Ann Arbor	MI	48105	313 677-1400 313 677-1465
EXCEL Midwest Women Business Owners Development Team	66 W. Lafayette	Detroit	MI	48226	313 961-4748 313 961-5434
EXCEL Seldman School of Business SBDC	301 W. Fulton Eberhard Center Room 716-S	Grand Rapids	MI	49504-6495	616 771-6693 616 771-6805
Grand Rapids Opportunities for Women (GROW)	25 Sheldon SE Suite 210	Grand Rapids	MI	49503	616 458-3404 678 458-6557
Women in New Development (WIND)	P.O. Box 579	Bemidji	MN	56601	218 751-4631 218 751-8452

ORGANIZATION NAME	ADDRESS	CITY	STATE	ZIP CODE	TEL/FAX#
Women's Business Center, White Earth Reservation Tribal Council	P.O. Box 478	Mahnomen	MN	56557	218 935-2827 218 935-2390
NAWBO	Suite 216	St. Louis	MO	6315	314 663-0046 314 863-2076
National Council of Negro Women	106 W. Green St.	Mount Bayou	MS	38762	601 741-3342 601 741-2195
Montana Women's Capital Fund	302 North Last Chance Gulch	Helena	MT	59624	406 443-3144 406 442-1789
Women's Opportunity and Resource Development Inc.	127 N. Higgins	Missoula	MT	59802	406 543-3550 406 721-4584
Women's Business Institute	P.O. Box 9238	Fargo	ND	58106-9238	701 235-6488 701 235-8284
NAWBO EXCEL	225 Hamilton St.	Bound Brook	NJ	0885-2042	908 560-9607 908 560-9687
Women's Economic Self-Sufficiency Team (WESST Corp.)	414 Silver Southwest	Albuquerque	NM	87102	505 241-4760 505 241-4766
Women's Economic Self-Sufficiency Team (WESST Corp.)	P.O. Box 5007 NDCBU	Taos	NM	87571	505 758-3099 505 758-3099
Women's Economic Self-Sufficiency Team (WESST Corp.)	691 South Telshor	Las Cruces	NM	88001	505 522-3707 505 522-4414
Women's Economic Self-Sufficiency Team (WESST Corp.)	500 West Main	Farmington	NM	87401	505 325-0678 505 325-0695
Nevada Self Employment Trust	1600 E. Desert Inn Road, #209E	Las Vegas	NV	89109	702 734-3555 702 734-3530
Nevada Self Employment Trust (Parent Organization)	560 Mill Street	Reno	NV	89502	702 329-6789 702 734-3530
American Woman's Economic Development Corp. (Parent Organization to AWED)	71 Vanderbilt Ave. Suite 320	New York	NY	10169	212 692-9100 212 688-2718
Asian Women in Business	134 Spring St. Suite 203	New York	NY	10012	212 226-1737 212 334-3158
EMPOWER Pyramid Career Services	2400 Cleveland Avenue NW	Canton	OH	44709	216 453-3767 216 453-6079
Enterprise Center/Women's Business Center	129 E. Main St.	Hillsboro	OH	45133	513 393-9599 513 393-8159
Greater Columbus Women's Business Initiative	37 North High St.	Columbus	OH	43215	614 2256082 614 469-8250

ORGANIZATION NAME	ADDRESS	CITY	STATE	ZIP CODE	TEL/FAX#
Northwest Ohio Women's Entrepreneurial Network	300 Madison Avenue Suite 200	Toledo	OH	43604	419 243-8191 419 241-8302
Ohio Women's Business Resource Network (OWBRN)	77 South High Street, 28th Floor	Columbus	OH	43266	614 466-2682 614 486-0829
Region IV Consortium	Wright State University SBDC College of Business 120 Rike Hall	Dayton	OH	45433	513 873-3503 513 873-3545
The Cushwa Center for Industrial Development, Youngstown State University	410 Wick Ave.	Youngstown	OH	44555-3495	216 742-3496 216 742-3784
Women Entrepreneurs, Inc.	P.O. Box 2662	Cincinnati	OH	45202	513 884-0700 513 665-2052
Women's Business Resource Program of SE Ohio	Technology & Enterprise Building 20 E. Circle Drive Suite 180	Athens	OH	457012	614 593-1797 614 593-1795
Women's Development Center Inc.	300 N. Abbe Rd.	Elyria	OH	44035	216 386=0770 216 366-0769
Women's Entrepreneurial Growth Organization (WEGO)	P.O. Box 544	Akron	OH	44309	216 972-5179 216 972-5513
Women's Network Inc.	1540 W. Market Street Suite 100	Akron	OH	44313	216 804-5636 216 864-6526
Working Women's Money University	3501 NW 63rd Suite 609	Oklahoma City	OK	73116	405 842-1196 405 842-5067
Southern Oregon Women's Access to Credit	33 North Central Suite 209	Medford	OR	97501	541 779-3992 541 779-5195
National Association of Women Business Owners	560 Solway St. Suite 207	Pittsburgh	PA	15217	412 521-4735 412 521-4737
Women's Business Development Center	1315 Walnut St. Suite 1116	Philadelphia	PA	19107	215 790-9232 215 790-9231
The Entrepreneur's Network for Women	P.O. Box 81	Watertown	SD	57201	605 82-5080 605 882-5069
Center for Women's Business Enterprise (CWBE)	2425 West Loop South Suite 1004	Houston	TX	77027	713 552-1267 713 578-7061
North Texas Women's Business Development Center, Inc.	1402 Corinth St.	Dallas	TX	75215-2111	214 428-1177 214 428-1197

ORGANIZATION NAME	ADDRESS	CITY	STATE	ZIP CODE	TEL/FAX#
Utah Technology Finance Corp.	177 E. 100 South	Salt Lake City	UT	84111	801 364-4346 801 364-4361
Women's Business Assistance Project/ NCAIED Pacific Region	1000 W. Harrison South Tower Suite 530	Seattle	WA	98119	206 285-2190 206 285-2870
Wisconsin Women Entrepreneurs, Inc.	6949 N. 100th St.	Milwaukee	WI	53224	414 358-9260 414 358-9261
Wisconsin Women's Business Initiative Corp. (WWBIC)	1915 N. Dr. Martin Luther King Jr. Drive	Milwaukee	WI	53212	414 372-2070 414 373-2083
Wisconsin Women's Business Initiative Corp.(WWBIC)	16 North Carrol Street Suite 310	Madison	WI	53703	608 257-7409 608 257-7429

CENTERS TO CALL

NAME	TEL NO./ADDRESS	NOTES

GOVERNMENT RESOURCES

SMALL BUSINESS ADMINISTRATION   800 827-5722
409 Third Street, NW, Washington, DC 20416
    The United States Small Business Administration (SBA) on line provides immediate access to information about SBA programs   URL http://www/sba/gov
    Almost all services and programs provided by the SBA are administered through the local branch/district offices. Contact the nearest district office or to find out if there is a nearby branch office call   (800) 827-5722

OFFICE OF WOMEN'S BUSINESS OWNERSHIP

DEMONSTRATION PROGRAM   202 205-6673
    Office of Women's Business Ownership is the primary advocate for the interests of women business owners and provides current and "wanna be" women business owners access to the following services and programs:
    ! Technical, financial, management information and workshops (usually free)
    ! Information on selling to the federal government
    ! A Women's Business Ownership Kit   http://www.onlinewbc.org

The Women's' Network for Entrepreneurial Training (WNET) matches successful entrepreneurial women (mentors) business owners with women business owners whose companies are ready to grow (protégés). Meeting one-on-one over a period of one year, mentors guide protégés through the process of achieving success in business.

PROCUREMENT ASSISTANCE

The Small Business Act of 1953 states that a fair proportion of government procurement should be placed with small firms. Contact the local SBA office for information on nearby procurement conferences or for a copy of information published on how to do business with the agency, contact the Office of Small and Disadvantage Utilization.

ASSISTANCE FOR MINORITIES & WOMEN

Office of Minority Enterprise Development   202 205-6410
    The main objective of this office is to foster business ownership by individuals who are socially and economically disadvantaged. SBA Management and Technical Assistance Program places grants, agreements and contracts with individuals and non-profit organizations to provide management and technical assistance to eligible recipients.

SBA – SERVICE CORP OF RETIRED EXECUTIVES (SCORE) 800 827-5722
    SCORE provides expert problem-solving assistance to small business and can advise you on tax filing requirements and how to comply.

SBA ONLINE 800 697-4636 900 463-4636

     The toll-free 800 number offers information on the SBA's loans and business development programs. The 900 number is 30 cents for the first minute, 10 cents for each additional minute, and allows users to communicate with each other and download information directly to their own computers.

OTHER RESOURCES FOR SMALL BUSINESS OWNERS

INTERNAL REVENUE SERVICE (IRS) 800 829-1040
1111 Constitution Avenue, NW
Washington, DC 20224
     The IRS Education department offers several programs and services, including the Small Business Tax Education Program. For information call the toll-free number listed above, or the IRS offices nearest you. Ask for the taxpayer education coordinator.
     For information on federal tax filing requirements and other questions related to federal tax obligations including tax forms call 800 829-3676

COPYRIGHTS, TRADEMARKS & PATENTS
Copyright Office 202 707-3000
Library of Congress, Washington, DC 20559 URL http//lcweb.loc.gov/copyright/
     Although registration is not necessary to claim copyright in an original, literary, dramatic, musical or artistic work, registration does provide certain benefits in the event of infringement. The copyright office can provide details on how to register a copyright. To order forms call 202 707-9100.
     ! Circular 1, Copyright Basics
     ! Circular 2, Publications on Copyright

STATE GOVERNMENT RESOURCES

There is a primary agency or office in each state that provides excellent, one-stop guidance on the programs and services offered to small business at the state level. These agencies or offices to meet the needs of individual firms by providing either direct assistance or by serving as an information clearinghouse. All resources available to small businesses are available to minority- and women-owned businesses. The following numbers are the lead State Government Resource for each state.

STATE	ADDRESS	TELEPHONE NUMBER	INTERNET ADDRESS
ALABAMA DEVELOPMENT OFFICE	401 Adams Avenue, Montgomery, AL. 36130-4106	(334) 242-0400	http://ww.ado.state.al.us
ALASKA DEPARTMENT OF COMMERCE & ECONOMIC DEVELOPMENT	State Office Building, Ninth Fl. 333 Willoughby Avenue, P.O. Box 110800, Juneau, AK. 99811-0800	(907) 465-2500	http://www.state.ak.us
ARIZONA BUSINESS DEVELOPMENT FINANCE CORPORATION	186 East Broadway Boulevard, Tucson, AZ 85701	(800) 264-3377	http://www/state.az.us/ep/
ARKANSAS INDUSTRIAL DEVELOPMENT COMMISSION	One State Capitol Mall, Little Rock, AR 72201	(501) 682-1121	http://www.aidc.state.ar.us
CALIFORNIA OFFICE OF SMALL BUSINESS	801 K Street, Suite 1700, Sacrament, CA 95814	(916) 324-1295	http://www.commerce.ca.gov
COLORADO OFFICE OF BUSINESS DEVELOPMENT	1625 Broadway, Suite 1710, Denver, CO 80202	(303) 892-3840	http://www.state.co.us/ gov_dir/obd/obd.htm
CONNECTICUT OFFICE OF SMALL BUSINESS SERVICES	865 Brook Street, Rocky Hill, CT 06067-34056	(860) 258-4200	http://www.state.ct.us/ ecd/index.html
DELAWARE ECONOMIC DEVELOPMENT OFFICE	99 Kings Highway, P.O. Box 1401, Dover, DE 19903	(302) 739-4271	http://www.state.de.us
DISTRICT OF COLUMBIA-OFFICE OF THE ASSISTANT CITY ADMIN. FOR ECONOMIC DEVELOPMENT	444 4TH Street, NW, Suite 1140, Washington, DC 20003	(202) 727-6365	http://www.ci.washington.dc.us/ DCRA/dcrahome.html

STATE	ADDRESS	TELEPHONE NUMBER	INTERNET ADDRESS
FLORIDA – ENTERPRISE FLORIDA	390 N. Orange Avenue, Suite 1300, Orlando, FL 32801	(407) 316-4600	http://www.state.fl.us/ commerce/
GEORGIA DEPARTMENT OF INDUSTRY, TRADE & TOURISM	P.O. Box 1776, Atlanta, GA. 30301	(404) 656-3545	http://www.gditt.com
HAWAII DEPARTMENT OF BUSINESS, ECONOMIC DEVELOPMENT & TOURISM	250 South Hotel Street, 5th Floor, Honolulu, HI 96813	(808) 586-2591	http://www.hawaii.gov /dbedt/
IDAHO DEPARTMENT OF COMMERCE	700 West State Street, P.O. Box 83720, Boise, ID 83720-2700	(208) 334-2470	http://www.idoc.state .id.us
ILLINOIS DEPARTMENT OF COMMERCE & COMMUNITY AFFAIRS	620 East Adams Street, Third Floor, Springfield, IL 62701	(217) 524-5856	http://www. ilcommerce.com
INDIANA STATE INFORMATION CENTER	402 West Washington Street, Room W160, Indianapolis, IN 46204	In State (800) 45-STATE	http://www.state.in. us
IOWA DEPARTMENT OF ECONOMIC DEVELOPMENT	200 East Grand Avenue, Des Moines, IA 50309	(515) 242-4700	http://www.state.ia. us/government/ided
KANSAS DEPARTMENT OF COMMERCE & HOUSING	700 SW Harrison Street, Suite 1300, Topeka, KS 66603-3712	(913) 296-3481	http://www.kcin. cecase.ukans.edu/
KENTUCKY CABINET FOR ECONOMIC DEVELOPMENT	2300 Capital Plaza Tower, Frankfort, KY 40601	(800) 626-2930	http://www.state.ky. us/edc/cabmain.htm
LOUISIANA DEPARTMENT OF ECONOMIC DEVELOPMENT	P.O. Box 94185, Baton Rouge, LA 70804-9185	(504) 342-3000	http://www.ided.state. la.us
MAINE DEPARTMENT OF ECONOMIC & COMMUNITY DEVELOPMENT	State House Station #59 Augusta, ME 04333-0949	(207) 287-2656	http://www.state.me. us/agencies.htm
MARYLAND DEPARTMENT OF BUSINESS & ECONOMIC DEVELOPMENT	Redwood Tower, 217 East Redwood Street, Baltimore, MD 21202	(410) 767-6300	http://www .mdbusiness.state.md .us

STATE	ADDRESS	TELEPHONE NUMBER	INTERNET ADDRESS
MASSACHUSETTS DEPARTMENT OF ECONOMIC DEVELOPMENT	One Ashburton Place, Room 2101, Boston, MA 02108	(617) 727-8380	http://www.state.ma.us/mobd
MICHIGAN JOBS COMMISSION	Victor Office Center, Fourth Floor, 201 N. Washington Square, Lansing, MI 49813	(517) 373-9808	http://www.mjc.state.mi. us
MINNESOTA SMALL BUSINESS ASSISTANCE OFFICE	500 Metro Square, 121 7th Place East, St. Paul, MN 55101-2146	(800) 657-3858	http://www.dted.state.mn.us/busasst/smbus/
MISSISSIPPI DEPARTMENT OF ECONOMIC & COMMUNITY DEVELOPMENT	P.O. Box 849, Jackson, MS 39205-0849	(601) 359-3449	http://www.decd.state.ms.us
MISSOURI DEPARTMENT OF ECONOMIC DEVELOPMENT	Truman State Office Building 301 West High Street, Rm. 680, P.O. Box 1157, Jefferson City, MO 65102	(573) 751-4962	http://www.ecodev.state.mo.us
MONTANA DEPARTMENT OF COMMERCE	1424 Ninth Avenue, Helena, MT 59620-0501	(406) 444-3494	http://www.mt.gov/gov/ gov.htm
NEBRASKA DEPARTMENT OF ECONOMIC DEVELOPMENT	P.O. Box 94666, 301 Centennial Mall South, Lincoln, NE 68509-4666	(402) 471-3747	http://www.ded.state.com.ne.us
NEVADA STATE DEVELOPMENT CORPORATION	350 South Center Street, Suite 310, Reno, NV 89501	(702) 323-3625	http://www.state.nv.us
NEW HAMPSHIRE BUSINESS FINANCE AUTHORITY	14 Dixon Avenue, Suite 101, Concord, NH 03301-4954	(603) 271-2391	http://www.state.nh.us/ bfa/bfa.htm
NEW JERSEY DEPARTMENT OF COMMERCE & ECONOMIC DEVELOPMENT	20 West State Street, CN 835, Trenton, NJ 08625	(609) 292-2444	http://www.state.nj.us/ business.htm
NEW MEXICO ECONOMIC DEVELOPMENT DEPARTMENT	P.O. Box 20003 Santa Fe, NM 87504-5003	(505) 827-0300	http://www.edd.state.nm.us

STATE	ADDRESS	TELEPHONE NUMBER	INTERNET ADDRESS
NEW YORK EMPIRE STATE DEVELOPMENT	633 Third Avenue, New York, NY 10017	(518) 283-1010	http://www.empire.state.ny.us
NORTH CAROLINA SMALL BUSINESS & TECHNOLOGY DEVELOPMENT CENTER	333 Fayetteville Street Mall, Raleigh, NC 27603	(919) 715-7272	http://www.state.us/business/
NORTH DAKOTA DEPARTMENT OF ECONOMIC DEVELOPMENT & FINANCE	1833 East Bismarck Expressway, Bismarck, ND 58504	(701) 328-5300	http://www.state.nd.us/edf/
OHIO OFFICE OF SMALL BUSINESS	77 South High Street, P.O. Box 1001, Columbus, OH 43216-1001	(614) 466-2718	http://www.ohiobiz.com
OKLAHOMA DEPARTMENT OF COMMERCE	900 N. Stiles, P.O. Box 26980, Oklahoma City, OK 73126-0980	(405) 815-6552	http://www.odoc.state.ok.us
OREGON ECONOMIC DEVELOPMENT OFFICE	775 Summer Street, NE, Salem, OR 97310	(503) 986-0123	http://www.econ.state.or.us
PENNSYLVANIA DEPARTMENT OF COMMUNITY & ECONOMIC DEVELOPMENT	374 Form Building, Harrisburg, PA 17120	(800) 280-3801	http://www.state.pa.us
PUERTO RICO DEPARTMENT OF ECONOMIC DEVELOPMENT & COMMERCE	P.O. Box 4435, San Juan, PR 00902-4435	(787) 721-2898	(NA)
RHODE ISLAND ECONOMIC DEVELOPMENT CORPORATION	One West Exchange Street, Providence, RI 02903	(401) 277-2601	http://www.riedc.com
SOUTH CAROLINA ENTERPRISE DEVELOPMENT, INC.	P.O. Box 1149, Columbia, SC 29202	(803) 252-8806	http://www.state.sc.us/commerce/
SOUTH DAKOTA GOVERNOR'S OFFICE OF ECONOMIC DEVELOPMENT	711 East Wells Avenue, Pierre, SD 57501-3369	(605) 773-5032	http://www.state.sd.us/stateexecutive/oed/oed.htm

STATE	ADDRESS	TELEPHONE NUMBER	INTERNET ADDRESS
TENNESSEE DEPARTMENT OF ECONOMIC & COMMUNITY DEVELOPMENT	320 Sixth Avenue North, Nashville, TN 37243	In-State (800) 872-7201	http://www.state.tn.us
TEXAS DEPARTMENT OF COMMERCE	1700 North Congress Avenue, P.O. Box 12728, Austin, TX 78711	(512) 936-0100	http://www.tdoc.state.tx. us
UTAH COMMUNITY & ECONOMIC DEVELOPMENT	324 South State Street, Suite 500, Salt Lake City, UT 84111	(801) 538-8700	http://www.ce.ex.state.tx.us
VERMONT DEPARTMENT OF ECONOMIC DEVELOPMENT	109 State Street, Montpelier, VT 05602	(802) 828-3211	http://www.state.vt.us/dca
VIRGINIA SMALL BUSINESS DEVELOPMENT NETWORK	P.O. Box 798, Richmond, VA 23218-0798	(804) 371-8253	http://www.state.va.us
WASHINGTON BUSINESS ASSISTANCE CENTER	906 Columbia Street SW, P.O. Box 48300, Olympia, WA 98504-8300	(360) 753-4900	http://www.wa.gov/commerce/html
WEST VIRGINIA DEVELOPMENT OFFICE	1900 Kanawha Blvd., E., Charleston, WV 25305-0311	(304) 558-2234	http://www.state.wv.us/wvdev
WISCONSIN DEPARTMENT OF DEVELOPMENT	123 West Washington Avenue, P.O. Box 7970, Madison, WI 53707	(608) 266-1018	http://www.badger.state.wi.us/agencies/commerce
WYOMING DIVISION OF ECONOMIC & COMMUNITY DEVELOPMENT	6101 Yellowstone Road, Fourth Floor, Cheyenne, WY 82002	(307) 777-7284	http://www.state.wy.us:80/commerce/decd/index.htm

ADDITIONAL CONTACTS

NAME	TELEPHONE NUMBER	NOTES

WISE AND SOMETIMES WACKY WORDS FROM CLOSE FRIENDS, CASUAL ACQUAINTANCES, FAMILY MEMBERS AND ANONYMOUS PEOPLE ON THE INTERNET (who, for the most part, provide solid business advice with their wisdom and wackiness)

Every woman should have a realization that she is actually going to have an old age and some money set aside to help fund it.

Every woman should know her childhood may not have been perfect, but it's over.

The Internet, via Lee Bright

From the Nepal Good Luck Tantra Totem:

Give people more than they expect and do it cheerfully.

Remember that love and great achievements involve great risks.

When you lose, don't lose the lesson.

Judge your success by what you had to give up in order to get it.

Mind your own business.

And from my pals:

Leap and the net will appear!
Carole Zavala Laidlaw

If asked to define myself, I would not describe my job, citizenship, race, gender, economic status, or health. I would do it all in one word: "fortunate".
Brian Toman

I don't have an inner child. She's always hanging out and the problem is getting her to behave.
Sue Richmond

Life is uncertain. We all know this. This is one of the many reasons why I like to eat dessert first. You never know. What we DO know is that whatever is happening, it won't last forever. Because life is about change.
Lee Bright (from her book "Get Over Yourself!")

You can't always choose your customers but you can choose your partners and co-workers. Choose ethics and compatibility with your own value system over smarts and all the "contacts" in the world.
Allison Sampson

Allison also says, "*Always have an exit strategy,*" a lesson learned, no doubt, during her tenure as a banker and as a producer of non-profit theater and dance. Needless to say, I agree passionately with both pieces of advice.

GETTING BY WITH A LITTLE HELP FROM MY FRIENDS

The people on the following pages have been invaluable in putting this book together. Since they may also be helpful to you as you build or expand your business or non-profit organization, I have included contact information next to their pictures.

Patti Koltnow
The Koltnow Group
323 461-1900
pkla@earthlink.net
Consultant to non-profit organizations.
Specializes in "start ups" and "turnarounds".

Adrienne Hall
The Hall Group
310 552-0068 aahall@earthlink.net
Advertising/Marketing; Organizational
Board Development; Venture Capital

Jeanie Barnett
Editor-In-Chief, MBE Magazine
310 540-9398
jeanieb@cruzio.com
Writer; Editor; Author;
Expert on Women's Issues

Dr. Marsha Firestone
President,
Women Presidents' Organization
333 Madison Avenue
New York, NY 10017
212 818-9424
Nationwide organization for
women CEOs and
entrepreneurs whose
businesses generate
more than $1 million annually.

Marryn Hann
ALW & Associates
562 433-3920
Project Management

Allison Sampson
310 573-0257
asampson@earthlink.net
Management Consultant; Strategist for non-profits

Janet Trondle
562 856-3765
j.trondle@att.net
Training; Human Resources Management;
Project Management

Carole Zavala Laidlaw
CZ & Associates
949 497-6397
Strategic Planning; Board Development, Fund Raising

Lindsey Johnson Suddarth
Co-CEO, Women Incorporated
213 680-3375
womeninc@aol.com
Access to capital and credit

Lindsay Shields
Partner, LJ Group
562 621-0521
Public Relations; Event Manager; Fund Raising

Lee Bright
Bright Marketing International
562 438-0217
LBright719@aol.com
Marketing; Public Relations;Training
(international clientele)

Hope Tschopik Schneider
Culture + Planning Group
818 790-4000
Strategic Planning; Organizational Assessment;
Board Development

and Marc Wilder
Vice President
Lar Holding
wildermarc@aol.com

Margo Upham
Upham & Associates
310 271-5745
margo4pr@aol.com
Public Relations; Media Consultant;
Event Management

ACKNOWLEDGMENTS

Many thanks to the National Network for Artist Placement (NNAP) for commissioning this book and for their confidence that I could deliver it. Their commitment to the welfare of artists is long-standing and *Breaking Through The Clutter* is the second book of mine they have published in their effort to help artists better understand the business side of art. I hope this time we got it right.

I also wish to thank a number of people without whom this book would not have seen the light of day. Janet Trondle worked on this publication at least as hard as I did. Her experience as a long time AT&T manager brought perspective to the chapters on personnel issues and business planning and if she had not stayed glued to the Internet for many days and nights, the Resource Section would have half the entries it now has.

Lindsay Shields and the LJ Group surveyed and talked to more than half the artists whose views inform all the chapters of this book. Marryn Hann checked hundreds of facts, phone numbers and e-mail addresses, and found the cover designer for *Breaking Through The Clutter*. Dr. Marsha Firestone, Margo Upham and Lee Bright generously allowed me to lift worksheets and charts from their own excellent publications and lesson plans. Hope Tschopik Schneider contributed a chapter on Planning only she could have written, and Kathleen Staunton valiantly reviewed the hundreds of pages of early drafts I sent to her written on paper napkins and recycled fax paper.

The amazing Jeanie Barnett used her impressive skills as an editor to ensure that neither the NNAP nor I would be embarrassed by dangling participles and phrases that would make a sailor blush. The salty language and danglers remaining are a product of my poor judgment rather than hers. My perky partner, Lindsey Johnson Suddarth, took time from an overdue and well-deserved vacation to write the Foreword. My husband, Marc Wilder, a man who thinks Kafka was a frivolous writer, manfully held his tongue while he read through long and silly lists of bad attitude bad asses and lunatics I had hired. I am grateful to him and to all my friends for their contributions, support and restraint.

I am also grateful to the artists and women entrepreneurs in America who, day by day, inspire millions of others throughout the world to believe in and follow their own dreams. Although a few of these remarkable people are mentioned (far too briefly) in this book, they all deserve to have volumes written about the miracles they achieve when they simply do their work.

We all get by with a little help from our friends and some of mine are pictured at the back of *Breaking Through The Clutter*. They and others too shy or too prudent to show their handsome faces have helped me move from the arts to business and on to some sort of hybrid lifestyle that incorporates both. In no particular order, although Scott and Kevin Emery and Marc Wilder are always first among equals, they are: John Suddarth,

Adrienne Hall, Amy Larkin, Rachel Bellow, Carole Zavala Laidlaw, Warren Christensen, Ron Noblet, Harry Newman and Patti Koltnow.

Finally, I wish to acknowledge and thank the people to whom this book is dedicated. Although the most affluent of the three will never give Midas a run for his money, each, at different times, for different reasons, has, with reckless sincerity, asked two seldom heard and dangerous questions. The first was: Do you need money? The second was: Do you need help baby-sitting? Allowing for the possibility of intoxication and madness at the time the questions were asked, I am nonetheless humbled by their generosity. And although the prospect of unsolicited, no-interest loans and quiet, child-free afternoons boggle the mind, their friendship boggles the mind, heart and soul and leaves me breathless.

The fact that I (and they) define friendship in such pragmatic terms also leaves me a little breathless. Twenty years ago I would have talked about friendship in terms of shared dreams and heartfelt discussions about Major Issues. These days I've come to understand that talk is usually cheap and talk about Major Issues, like Art for Art's sake, is an indulgence of the well-fed. Dreams, of course, are still seductive, and sharing a dream will always be a miracle. But an offer of free baby-sitting when your husband is sick and your desk is overflowing with overdue work assignments? That deserves an X-File investigation. It certainly warrants revisiting one's definition of friendship.

Susie, Brian and Allison, steadfast friends, loyal and true. Thank you for giving shape to the purest art form of all.